TOM SPERLINGER
JOSIE MCLELLAN
RICHARD PETTIGRE

WHO ARE UNIVERSITIES FOR?

Re-making higher education

BRISTOL
UNIVERSITY
PRESS

First published in Great Britain in 2018 by

Bristol University Press
University of Bristol
1-9 Old Park Hill
Bristol
BS2 8BB
UK
t: +44 (0)117 954 5940
www.bristoluniversitypress.co.uk

North America office:
Bristol University Press
c/o The University of Chicago Press
1427 East 60th Street
Chicago, IL 60637, USA
t: +1 773 702 7700
f: +1 773 702 9756
sales@press.uchicago.edu
www.press.uchicago.edu

© Bristol University Press 2018

British Library Cataloguing in Publication Data
A catalogue record for this book is available from the British Library.

Library of Congress Cataloging-in-Publication Data
A catalog record for this book has been requested.

ISBN 978-1-5292-0038-6 (paperback)
ISBN 978-1-5292-0040-9 (ePub)
ISBN 978-1-5292-0041-6 (Mobi)
ISBN 978-1-5292-0039-3 (ePDF)

The right of Tom Sperlinger, Josie McLellan and Richard Pettigrew to be identified as authors of this work has been asserted by them in accordance with the Copyright, Designs and Patents Act 1988.

The statements and opinions contained within this publication are solely those of the authors and not of the University of Bristol or Bristol University Press. The University of Bristol and Bristol University Press disclaim responsibility for any injury to persons or property resulting from any material published in this publication.

Bristol University Press works to counter discrimination on grounds of gender, race, disability, age and sexuality.

Cover design by blu inc, Bristol
Front cover: image kindly supplied by Thierry Bal and Europa
Printed and bound in Great Britain by CMP, Poole
Bristol University Press uses environmentally responsible print partners

for our students

As first-degree granting colleges ... we tend to accept the standing acceptance procedure, thereby reinforcing the inequalities that already exist [in society], oblivious to the plight of an unquantified number of disadvantaged individuals, and to the right to education we claim they have.

Sari Nusseibeh (2014, p 9)

Democracy will realize itself – if it does – in our *whole* society and our *whole* culture: and, for this to happen, the universities need the abrasion of different worlds of experience, in which ideas are brought to the test of life.

E.P. Thompson (1997, p 30, emphasis in original)

The university I have been trying to imagine does not seem to me utopian, though the problems and contradictions to be faced in its actual transformation are of course real and severe.

Adrienne Rich (1979, p 153)

Contents

Authors' note

The book was conceived and planned by Josie McLellan and Tom Sperlinger, and written with Richard Pettigrew. It draws on experiences that the three of us have had as course directors for a Foundation Year in Arts and Humanities at the University of Bristol, which is discussed in these pages. We have debated the issues in this book in our work and teaching practice, and we hope that a sense of dialogue – with colleagues and students – is evident in what follows, and that it adds to the argument the book makes for a more collaborative higher education system. We are grateful to those students and colleagues who have agreed to be quoted, some of whose names and details have been changed with agreement. The narrative 'I' in the book indicates a different author at various points; for example, the family history in the opening pages belongs to Tom Sperlinger, while the first-person accounts of industrial action in the conclusion are by Josie McLellan.

Acknowledgements

We would like to thank Tom Flynn, Erika Hanna and Emily Tiplady for their comments on an early proposal for this project. We were fortunate to have readers of the full manuscript who were generous with their time and expertise, while also being incisive in their comments: our heartfelt thanks to Lorna Henry, Zoë Pither, Alan Tuckett and Sorana Vieru, all of whom shaped the final book in significant ways. Mwenza Blell and Max Kenner shared their experiences with us and have allowed us to draw on their ideas. An earlier version of the introduction was presented as a research paper for the Centre for Knowledge, Culture and Society in the School of Education at the University of Bristol in January 2018. We are grateful to Keri Facer for the invitation to speak and to all those who asked helpful questions, including Cassie Earl, Mhemooda Malek, Helen Manchester and Julia Paulson. Fran Johnson gave us permission to draw on published and forthcoming research she completed after interviewing students at Bristol as part of a project commissioned by the Office for Fair Access, which was led by John Butcher at the Open University. Anthea Sperlinger encouraged us to tell Lizzie Brown's story and Maura Tierney at the National University of Ireland provided documents relating to Lizzie's degree. We are grateful to all at Bristol University Press for their advice and encouragement. We dedicate this book to all of our students, who have taught us so much, and in particular to those who have learned together with us on the BA in English Literature and Community Engagement and the Foundation Year in Arts and Humanities at the University of Bristol.

INTRODUCTION

Who are universities for?

In the early summer of 1904, Elizabeth Frances Brown, who was known in her family as Lizzie, travelled from Belfast to Dublin for her graduation ceremony. She was nearly 29, and had been studying for a degree since 1894. The ceremony was held at Trinity College, Dublin, but Lizzie's degree was awarded by the Royal University of Ireland (RUI), and she completed it by correspondence. She had paid £1 to be entered for her final examinations – in English, French and German Literature – and £2, having satisfied the examiners, to be admitted to the degree. The journey, perhaps by train, must have been an additional expense. There is no record of whether Lizzie's family travelled with her for the ceremony, or if there was a party at home in Belfast. There is a traditional graduation photograph: Lizzie is wearing a gown and a cap, perched on thick waves of hair. The back of an ornate chair is evident behind her. She looks almost at the camera, but slightly past it as well.

James Joyce's novel *Ulysses*, which is set on 16 June 1904 in Dublin, records that there was a 'prolonged summer drouth' that year and that water levels were low. I like to imagine that Lizzie's graduation took place on a sunny day. But Joyce's weather was a touch of fiction. Gifford and Seidman (2008) suggest it was 'normal Irish weather' in 1904, and 'far from dry' (p 569).

I have inherited three books from Lizzie, who was my great-grandmother, which are bound in red or brown leather that is now slightly worn at the edges. They are collections of poems by Walter Scott, Lord Tennyson and Robert Browning. In the front of each one is a card stating that the book was awarded as a school prize at Victoria College in Belfast, in 1890, 1891 and 1892 respectively. The school crest is embossed on the leather cover of each book. The cards state that the recipient, 'E.F. Brown', was awarded first place in her class in each year.

Lizzie was from a relatively poor family, all five of whose children were educated, including both of the girls and a son, Alf, whose legs were paralysed and who was carried to school by his siblings. He later became an architect. However, it was only the eldest son, Walter, who enrolled full-time at university, to study medicine. The family could not afford to fund more than one full-time student.

There are mysteries about Lizzie's story, one of which is why she wanted to study for a degree, and what it was for in her eyes. She worked in England and in Germany in her twenties, including as a governess and in the post office. It is possible she worked in part to fund her studies, but also that she wished to have a career. Lizzie's sister, Isabel, trained as a nurse in Portsmouth and returned to work as a nursing sister at the Royal Victoria Hospital in Belfast.

In her early thirties, Lizzie married James Johnstone, a pawnbroker, whom she knew from church. They had three children, the youngest of whom was my grandmother, Eilish. I have inherited Lizzie's piano, which we think came from James's shop. One of the few things I remember Eilish saying about her mother is that, after James died, Lizzie would leave her three young children with 'anyone she could find', so that she could go to the library and read.

★

This is a story about what it is like to enter a system that is not designed for you. The RUI admitted women from its inception in 1879, but it was an examining body, offering a form of award by correspondence without any direct teaching. Judith Harford (2008) notes that the RUI represented 'an olive branch' amid ongoing debates about university participation for Catholics in Ireland (p 46). Lizzie (who was Protestant) thus studied part-time by correspondence 'outside' the mainstream system, alongside many others. The situation was changing slowly by the time Lizzie graduated:

> In 1904, women finally gained admission to Trinity College Dublin following decades of trenchant opposition. However, their integration into the college, like their admission, was slow, first securing access to degrees in arts and medicine and later to more traditionally male fields like engineering. They were prohibited from residing in the college and were expected to leave the campus by six each evening. They accounted for about 15% of the student cohort by 1914, coming predominantly from Protestant middle-class and professional families. (Harford, pp 50-1)

This book is about the ways in which universities still include some groups and exclude others, an issue that affects institutions around the globe. It is also about the forms of learning that exist beyond them because of this: Eilish's memory of her mother, for example, suggests that Lizzie later turned to a library as what Adrienne Rich (1979) has called an 'unofficial university-without-walls' (p 127). Our hope is to reimagine who universities are 'for', and we argue that this has wide-ranging implications for the structure, content and experience of higher education.

Lizzie's story is historically and geographically specific. Indeed, it is tempting to see it as so distanced from us in time that it reads almost as fiction, because the conditions of who enters university and on what terms have changed dramatically since 1904. It is true that, as a high academic achiever at school, a young woman in Lizzie's social position in the UK would have many more opportunities to enter full-time higher education in 2018 than she did in 1894. Around the world too, about the same number of women study for an undergraduate degree as men, although women are a smaller proportion (44%) of those studying at doctorate level, according to a recent report by the United Nations Educational, Scientific and Cultural Organization (UNESCO, 2017, p 3). While access to higher education has improved for women, gender equality within the system remains elusive; the proportion of women continues to decline at each stage of the system up to professorial level. Meanwhile, in low income countries, only one third of 3.3 million undergraduates are women (UNESCO, 2017, p 3). There are various contexts in which Lizzie's story may still feel contemporary.

Moreover, Lizzie as she was on her graduation day – a lower middle-class woman in her late twenties, studying part-time – represents a segment of the population that is still dramatically and routinely excluded from universities in the UK. There has been a 61% drop in the number of part-time students in England since 2010, with women from less privileged backgrounds among those most affected (UK Parliament, House of Commons, 2018, p 4). There has been a fall in other regions too, although it is less dramatic. In Northern Ireland, which includes the area where Lizzie lived, there was a 5% drop in part-time entrants between 2012 and 2013 (p 25) while wider adult education provision has withered, with the regional Workers' Educational Association (WEA) closing altogether (BBC, 2014). Economic factors continue to push adults out of the region for employment, as, temporarily, in Lizzie's case: Northern Ireland has the slowest economic growth rate in the UK and its economy is predicted to dip between 8% and 12% after the 2019 exit from the European Union (UK Parliament,

House of Commons Exiting the European Union Committee, 2018, p 23).

Family expectations and circumstances continue to shape participation as well. We have lost the family thread that might tell us more about Lizzie's parents, but they must have been unusual for their time and class in encouraging all of their children to be educated and to travel. Many students still do pioneering work, as Lizzie did, as the first generation in their family to attend university, a privilege that comes with costs as well as rewards. An report by the Organisation for Economic Co-operation and Development in 2013 showed that, among its member countries, students from 'more educated families' were more than twice as likely to attend university (cited in O'Shea, 2016, p 61). In contrast, I write as someone from the fourth generation of my family to attend university. Higher education remains the norm for some families and communities, but not for others. The UK system also remains remarkably unresponsive to the shape of individual lives and the ways that circumstances may interrupt someone's education. When James Johnstone died, his children stopped going to school for several years, with lasting effects, although Eilish did go to agricultural college as a young woman. In the present day, it can still be peculiarly hard for someone to recover lost ground if their school life is interrupted.

Palfreyman and Temple (2017) estimate that there are now over 150 million students in higher education across 17,000 institutions around the world (p 2). Yet across the globe, as UNESCO (2017) has shown, participation is still determined and segregated along lines of geography, class and ethnicity. The poorest sectors of the population, indigenous groups and ethnic minorities participate at much lower rates than their peers. One in six Africans and Coloureds in South Africa attends higher education, compared with half of Whites (the terms given are those used in UNESCO's classification). Only 1% of the indigenous population in Mexico goes to university (pp 3-4).

In the UK, nearly three quarters of the richest 25- to 29-year-olds had completed four years of tertiary education in 2008-14, but only a third of the poorest (p 3). There are consistent trends in participation across the world, although it is worth noting that they also mask some differences in national, regional and institutional contexts. For example, the extent to which university is seen as a middle-class 'rite of passage' or as open to working-class communities varies at different universities in the UK.[1] Many communities, moreover, have self-organised outside the system. Jonathan Rose (2001) and others have shown the sheer extent of organised working-class intellectual life in the UK, for example.

There is also substantial evidence that students from groups that have been routinely excluded from universities continue to feel like outsiders within some institutions. Lizzie's experience as an 'external' student has its modern equivalents. In the UK, statistics from the Office for Fair Access (OFFA, 'Topic briefing: BME students', undated) show that retention rates are lower for all ethnic groups (except students of Chinese and Indian ethnicity) compared with their White peers, and degree outcomes are dramatically different for Black students regardless of entry requirements for their degrees and of the qualifications they had gained beforehand. These patterns of participation have implications not only for the individuals and communities concerned, but also for the kinds of knowledge and experience that universities miss out on or mishear. While the structures of higher education continue to assume a particular (White, male and/or middle-class) student, anyone who does not conform to this expectation may find it difficult to shape the knowledge that is being created as well as to benefit from it.

Jana Bacevic (2018) has noted that there has been a 'veritable "boom" in writing about the fate and future of higher education' in the UK in recent years. This includes works by David Willetts (2017), a former government minister for universities and science; by academics, such as Stefan Collini (2012); and by those half in- and half outside the system, like the journalist and researcher Andrew McGettigan (2013). These studies tend to focus, as Bacevic notes, mainly on critique of the current system. The focus also tends to be on a very particular set of issues, as in discussions on campuses and in the media, including whether universities are too commercialised or too remote from the rest of society, and (related to that) whether student fees have been a success, are too high, or should be abolished altogether. Most commentators assume that a 'university education' concerns primarily young, full-time students, although Willetts is frank about his regrets that the substantial decline in part-time study happened during his period in government (p 87). When access to universities is mentioned, it is seen largely as a success story (because of the greater number of students in the system than 20 years ago), or features what Bacevic notes as 'Oxbridge bashing'; for example, concerns have been expressed repeatedly over the very small number of Black and minority ethnic students at Cambridge and Oxford (Rustin, 2011). Within universities themselves, many of the debates position the 1970s as a sort of 'golden era' when grants were available and there were no fees, access was widening through new universities such as Sussex and East Anglia and the Open University, and government intervention in the system remained limited.

We share some of the fears articulated by others who have written about the future of higher education. Universities are facing a crisis of public confidence both as institutions and as symbols of expertise. However, it is our contention that we need a much more radical rethink of the form and structure of the higher education system if this crisis is to be addressed. In particular, we suggest a shift away from the norm of full-time study over three years at the age of 18. This model emerged in an era when the student population was dramatically smaller, and the nature of professional life was very different. A critical debate about whether it is still fit for purpose is long overdue. Indeed, the decline in part-time study comes at a time when the fourth industrial revolution will create unprecedented demand on those already in work to retrain and acquire new skills. In this context of rapid technological and economic change, it makes little sense to concentrate all of an individual's higher education into a brief period at the beginning of their lives. A report by the World Economic Forum (WEF, 2017) notes that:

> Over one in four adults surveyed in the OECD reported a mismatch between their current skills and the qualifications required for their jobs. Furthermore, approximately 35% of the skills demanded for jobs across industries will change by 2020. (p 1)

The pace of change is likely to accelerate and to create extreme inequality between those with high-skilled and high-paid jobs and those in low-skilled professions (Schwab, 2016). In other words, those without access to further and higher education will be left further behind economically. What is more, those workers who have already exhausted their entitlement to three years of full-time study will be unable to retrain as and when their current skills are outpaced by technological change.

It can be surprising how deeply ingrained assumptions are about who university is 'for'. In our teaching we sometimes give students an exercise in which they are asked to imagine 'a student' and a 'non-student'. No matter how varied the individuals completing the exercise, the assumption almost always emerges that a university student is someone who is aged between 18 and 21, who achieved high grades at school, who may be from a 'better' social class and who is likely to be White. The student is often female, and it is probable this assumption would have been different 50 or 100 years ago, as Lizzie Brown's story illustrates. There tend to be more varied examples of a 'non-student'. This might be someone who is highly successful but has taught themselves entirely through their employment, or it might be someone who is illiterate and thus shut out from an increasingly text-centred society. Often, this person sounds like someone who enjoys learning, but who has not found educational institutions inclusive or helpful.

These pictures are not mere caricatures. The undergraduate population in England is heavily biased towards 18-year-old entrants from higher socioeconomic groups in the south, while a 'mature' student today is much more likely to be aged between 21 and 30 than in middle-age (OFFA, 'Topic briefing: mature learners', undated). There are also particularly acute differences in participation between different types of institution, with disadvantaged groups disproportionately represented at non-elite, regional and post-1992 universities. As Vikki Boliver (2013) has shown, working-class and state-school students are much less likely to apply to the highly selective Russell Group of 24 universities (of which our own is a member, and about which we say more later), and those Black and Asian students who do apply to the Russell Group are much less likely to receive an offer than White and privately educated applicants with the same qualifications. 'Oxbridge bashing' is simplistic, but there are real issues about access across the full range of elite universities. As Lizzie's story and the statistics already cited illustrate, higher education systems tend to be structured around forms of exclusion: of women, working-class people, ethnic minorities, people with disabilities and those experiencing intersectional forms of disadvantage (so that there remain striking differences between different ethnic groups, for example, sometimes intersecting with class). Thus, even as universities expand, they reproduce those barriers in their entry requirements, admissions procedure, curricula and modes of study.

Sometimes the barriers that remain are harder to see at a first glance: for example, the way in which academic structures still implicitly cater for men, even though women now make up the majority of students. In another exercise, we asked a group of mature students to critique several films that different universities used to promote themselves to potential applicants on their websites. Among the general trends that the students noted was a bias towards disciplines that were performative: those involving rocket launches, scientific experiments (preferably exploding), or music or drama. By contrast, there were very few books depicted. In terms of gender, there was an implicit assumption that the student to whom the film was directed was male, especially in the presentation of sports (men playing rugby was a popular portrayal). One female student in her forties pointed out the phallic nature of many scenes in one film: all those rockets launching, test tubes overflowing, shots of tall university towers.

It is often argued that higher education should not be used as 'social engineering', and cannot fix the inequalities that may affect admission to it. Others claim that, with higher rates of young people now attending university, issues of 'access' are being addressed. It is true that a much higher proportion of young people now enter higher education. But as Richard Taylor (2009) has argued, in a critique of New Labour's education policies:

> There has been, undoubtedly, a rapid increase in the numbers of students in higher education, but the expansion has occurred very largely through greater participation from the higher socio-economic groups – 'more of the same' to put it crudely.... So, *widening* participation in addition to *increasing* participation has been only partially achieved. (p 74)

More recently, there has been near consensus across the political spectrum about the need for 'social mobility', yet relatively little interest in addressing the structural ways in which universities include some and exclude others. In a discussion about whether a 'centrist' policy is possible, Bacevic (2018) notes:

Any approach to higher education that does not first address longer-term social inequalities is unlikely to work; in periods of economic contraction, such as the one Britain is facing, it is even prone to backfire. Education policies, fundamentally, can do two things: one is to change how things are; the other is to make sure they stay the same. Arguing for a 'sensible' solution usually ends up doing the latter.

We contend, as Bacevic does, that we need to change 'how things are', rather than looking back nostalgically to an earlier era of higher education. We suggest participation should be reoriented across the course of a person's life, with a much larger percentage of the population engaging with and studying at universities at different points in their lives and for varying lengths of time and purposes. Such a change to the structure of universities would reset the debates about who pays for universities (and how) and their relevance as institutions to wider society. One of the arguments that is often made for tuition fees is that those who benefit from a university education should pay for it, rather than the cost being shared equally with those who do not attend. We wish to imagine a system in which the benefits would be shared much more widely.

As things stand, the rhetoric of widening access in itself reinforces social segregation and perpetuates the barriers that exclude some individuals from higher education. It is worth quoting Wendy Piatt, the former director general of the Russell Group (a self-selection of 24 research-intensive UK universities, often deemed an 'elite'), from a response to a 2013 Sutton Trust report on access to leading universities:

As this report shows the main reason pupils from disadvantaged backgrounds are less likely to go to leading universities is because they are not achieving the right grades. But students not only need good grades, they need them in the right subjects. This is especially important because entry into some courses, like Medicine or English, is very competitive. It is also the case that some very bright students are not encouraged to apply for leading universities. We cannot offer places to those who do not apply or who have not done the right subjects to study their chosen course. Access is an issue for leading universities across the globe – there is no silver bullet to this entrenched problem. School attainment, advice and aspirations must all be dramatically improved if we are to tackle the real barriers to fair access.

All Russell Group universities want to give places to students with the qualifications, potential and determination to succeed, irrespective of their background. We work hard to tackle the access gap. That's why we are pumping millions more into outreach programmes, why we published Informed Choices to give better guidance to students choosing their A-levels and it's why many of our universities sponsor academies and work with their local schools. (Russell Group, 2013)

University access is framed in this statement as an intractable problem and one that is faced by 'universities around the globe'. This implies that there are few or no solutions to the difficulty, and certainly none that universities themselves have readily to hand. Piatt frames the problem as being created by students (who do not get the 'right' grades in the 'right' subjects), by teachers or parents (who do not encourage the students to apply to 'leading' universities), and by schools' work on 'attainment, advice and aspirations'. It is striking that in this analysis only schools and A-Levels are mentioned and the focus is on young people; other qualifications, such as Access courses or BTECs are not mentioned, nor are mature students. In Piatt's analysis, the university's role is thus limited: it can offer outreach, provide information and sponsor schools, but it can only 'give' places on the basis of qualifications and to those 'determined to succeed'. In Chapter 5, we address the question of what prior qualifications are required to enter higher education. But it is worth noting here that while Piatt's statement is rhetorically about widening access, it is in fact about policing the borders of who gets in and out.

In a recent study of working-class education, *Miseducated*, Diane Reay (2017) argues that:

> Now that we have moved to a mass system of higher education, the logic of 'the educational ladder' ... has simply moved upwards. Instead of the 11-plus operating as a mechanism of social selection it is our elite universities that have taken over this role. (p 178)

In Sol Gamsu's (2015) words, 'The class elitism inherent in the logic of "raising up" a gifted few ... has returned with a vengeance in the widening participation discourse at elite universities.' Piatt's statement supports this analysis: it implies a system in which a small number of individual students can change how they 'perform' in order to enter the system. But the pressure is on them to perform and conform; universities themselves are not required to change. Reay is damning more widely about the progress that has been made towards real equality in all parts of the education system:

> The rhetoric of equality, fairness and freedom in education has intensified since the beginning of this century, but it has done so against a back-drop of ever-increasing inequalities, the entrenchment of neoliberalism and class domination. It is predominantly babble. (2017, p 185)

What would a different model of access look like, and who would benefit?

It is central to our argument that the changes we are proposing would produce a better system for *everyone*. Too often, widening access to universities is presented – as by Piatt – as an altruistic activity that universities do for philanthropic reasons. This produces a system in which lucky individuals are picked out of their own context and must conform to a set of institutional norms that are alien to them (often with painful results, as we discuss in Chapter 3). The dangers of this model of access run much deeper. Once a mass higher education system is created, as it has been in the UK over the past 20 years, it can lead to a deep schism in society between those inside and outside the system. This has implications for how democracy functions, as E.P. Thompson implies in the epigraph we have taken for this book. Arjun Appadurai warned in 2000:

> In the public spheres of many societies there is concern that policy debates occurring around world trade, copyright, environment, science and technology set the stage for life-and-death decisions for ordinary farmers, vendors, slum-dwellers, merchants and urban populations. And running through these debates is the sense that social exclusion is ever more tied to epistemic exclusion and concern that the discourses of expertise that are setting the rules for global transactions, even in the most progressive parts of the international system, have left ordinary people outside and behind. (p 2)

What would it mean for universities to be spaces where all those currently least likely to become undergraduates participated in higher education as a matter of course and on their own terms? Is this achievable and what would be the implications, both in the structure of those institutions and in the nature of the questions they would ask? This means thinking more radically about who is included in the creation of knowledge at universities from the ground up, and how the structures at every level work to support this inclusion. For all the attempts that have been made to transform UK universities so that they function on a narrow business model, they retain the vestiges of democratic structures of representation and inclusion. If we thus change who is in the university, we change what the university is, as well as what and who it is for. A different system would thus continually modify and reinvent itself, as different people participate in it.

We argue that those already in the higher education system would benefit from the changes we propose, as would universities, across the full spectrum of their activities from teaching to research and innovation. A crisis of trust in universities and in expertise has been recognised for some time. Universities and the UK funding councils for research have made enormous efforts to put 'public engagement' at the centre of research, an agenda that was driven initially by fear that key scientific advances had failed to gain public trust, as was evident in periodic crises about issues such as genetically modified crops and the vaccination of infants. (See NCCPE [undated] for a history of the term and McLennan [2008] for a sceptical view.) Yet these efforts at engagement often construct 'the public' as remaining *outside* the university. Meanwhile, the university classroom remains a space in which only a limited range of voices can participate on equal terms. These tensions are faced by institutions around the world, not only in the UK, as Appadurai's remarks make clear. They are embodied by the schisms that have emerged in local communities in California that border with Stanford University and the tech giants of Silicon Valley. In a 2014 article for the student newspaper, *The Stanford Daily*, titled 'The fight for East Palo Alto: where does Stanford lie?', Neil Chaudhary wrote:

Drive down University Avenue long enough and, at some point, you will notice a difference. On the Palo Alto side, there are clean streets, expensive cars, posh boutiques, and vagrancy laws. Now, go past the Highway 101 Bridge. You'll find East Palo Alto (EPA): dilapidated buildings and barren fields defined by artful graffiti, ethnic diversity and vibrant community stores. There is a clear divide separating the two worlds and along the front lines, a war of gentrification is being waged. At the heart of this struggle is the fight for affordable housing in EPA: a dwindling resource that will soon be eliminated by the encroaching demand for land in Silicon Valley.

This is a vivid illustration of how the division between universities and the cities in which they are situated – often characterised in the past as a split between 'town' and 'gown' – may be remade in devastating terms for a new era. As Chaudhary makes clear, the divide is partly one of ethnicity: 64.5% of East Palo Alto's 29,000 residents are Latino or Hispanic, 16.7% are Black, and 10% are Asian or Pacific Islander. The 'two worlds' of Palo Alto are a local example of what Appadurai warned about: universities are contributing to a growing schism, in many societies, between those living well in a global economy and others who are struggling to survive.

The questions posed by this book are also about how universities can respond to changing global circumstances. There is increasing tension between local/national and global/supra-national systems, symbolised in the UK rejection of the European Union and President Trump's America First policies, and foreseen much earlier by Appadurai and others. There are nonetheless ways in which universities might reconcile the longstanding pressures on them to be both local and global institutions. This would involve a reorientation of the university away from modes of exclusion, as symbolised in the case of East Palo Alto or the rhetoric of the Russell Group, and away from models of colonialism and domination. A radical model of inclusivity would also transform the production of knowledge, by opening the doors of the university to forms and communities of knowledge currently outside the artificial borders of academia. The idea that knowledge is at its richest when it is 'co-produced' is often credited to the political economist Elinor Ostrom. Ostrom's work asked why crime went up in Chicago in the 1970s. Her hypothesis was that when police began to patrol in cars rather than on foot, they lost the deep knowledge and awareness of neighbourhoods that had previously been co-produced with the community members they had met on their daily beat (NEF, 2008, p 9). Similarly, academic researchers are often unaware of the knowledge that exists outside universities, and the potential for collaboration with non-academic experts of different kinds.

Higher education can also help redefine the relationship between the Global South and North. Recently, universities saw skirmishes about the statues of Cecil Rhodes, ardent colonialist and educational philanthropist, that stand on their campuses. These clashes make manifest much deeper issues about who participates in the creation of knowledge and where that knowledge creation is 'centred'. These debates, we argue, are not in conflict with but analogous to how universities might tackle the growing inequalities and economic insecurities that exist on their own doorsteps. By creating new forms of participation that involve their local communities, rather than leaving them outside and behind, universities can work towards education as what Freire (1993) called the 'practice of freedom' rather than a practice of domination (p 93). They might also thus start to function in ways that resist what Gayatri Chakravorty Spivak (1988) calls 'epistemic violence' – the destruction or undermining of non-Western, or otherwise 'subaltern', forms of knowledge – on a wider scale (p 280).

★

This book argues that we need to remake higher education so that it is more responsive to the shape of a wider range of people's lives and that this would benefit students, universities and their staff, employers, and wider society. The arguments we make are not new, and we draw on real examples of practice locally and from further afield, as well as from theories from a variety of contexts. We hope to remake the case for a different system with new urgency and that this case may reach new audiences.

One of the challenges in the current higher education system is that those of us within or familiar with the system tend to talk to ourselves. This is a particular problem given that when debates about universities become visible in the public sphere, they often re-enforce a perception of higher education as exclusive or exclusionary; for example, in stories about racism and admissions at Oxbridge, vice-chancellors' pay, or admissions criteria. In imagining a reader for this book, we have tried to envisage a range of individuals who might currently think universities are not for them, or who have found it difficult to access the system from the margins. We hope that a contemporary reader in a position that echoes Lizzie Brown's might read this book and find it useful. We hope too it may be read by teachers and head-teachers, parents or prospective students, a community educator, or a current university teacher, student, administrator, staff member, or vice-chancellor. For that reason, among others, the book aims to make practical suggestions both about how the system as a whole can be transformed and what individuals and institutions can do, in the short term, to reform it.

Throughout the chapters that follow, we draw on our experiences of working within the system. We are three academics working at one Russell Group institution in England, the University of Bristol. Tom Sperlinger taught initially in adult education in Liverpool and came to Bristol's English Department in 2004, inheriting a programme of short courses that had originally been housed in a Department for Continuing Education (which closed in 1998). He designed and set up the part-time BA in English Literature and Community Engagement in 2008, a course taught one evening per week and in which each student creates a community project as part of their studies, which is discussed at various points through the book. Richard Pettigrew is a philosopher, with interests that cross over into Maths, who, with Sperlinger, designed the Foundation Year in Arts and Humanities, which commenced in 2013. It is a one-year, pre-degree course that does not require any prior qualifications. The programme (which is discussed in more depth in Chapter 3) is interdisciplinary, with two period modules structured around the question 'What does it mean to be human?', plus a study skills module and an individual project, in which students specialise in the area to which they plan to go on to a degree. Josie McLellan, who is a historian with a particular interest in co-producing research with people outside the academy, was one of the course directors from when the course started in 2013 and set up some of the first taster courses for the programme that were run with local communities, one of which she taught with the local Single Parent Action Network.

In drawing on our experiences, we speak from a part of the sector that has had a relatively poor track record in recent times of recruiting part-time and older students of the kind that are central to our argument. In 2016, some Russell Group institutions admitted no working-class mature students while the Open University admitted more than 700 (HESA, 2018). Colleagues in post-1992 universities and the further education sector would be justified in raising a sceptical eyebrow at three academics from the Russell Group proposing reforms to the sector that call for changes that mirror the work that their institutions do as a matter of course. However, this division in the sector is one of the issues we address. It is vital that reform is supported and initiated in the 'elite' areas of the sector, rather than being reluctantly conceded or resisted there. Penny Jane Burke, in *The Right to Higher Education* (2012), notes that:

> One of the most challenging aspects of this [work] is to involve those in the most privileged social positions, for example those in senior positions in prestigious universities, to participate in the questioning of practices and policies

that reinforce inequalities, differences and misrecognitions across a range of higher educational contexts. (p 190)

Our hope is that this book participates in that process, in which many colleagues across the sector are already engaged, and that a diverse range of readers find something they recognise in these pages.

1

Towards a university for everyone: some proposals

In her essay 'Towards a woman-centred university', Adrienne Rich (1979) notes that she is concerned 'not with an ideal future, but with some paths towards it' (p 147). In this chapter, we summarise our proposals, which are made in the same spirit. Most of these suggestions are explored at greater length in the chapters that follow. We say more about funding in this chapter, because it is so central to debates about higher education in the UK at present, but also because it can obscure equally important issues. Our hope, having addressed a funding model here, is to create space for other questions.

There have been a number of attempts recently to think about how we can 'ensure higher education leaves nobody behind', as it was articulated in a recent report by UNESCO (2017). Indeed, Penny Jane Burke's idea of a 'right' to higher education (2012) is increasingly becoming a reality:

> Ecuador and Greece are constitutionally bound to provide free post-secondary education to all citizens, while Tunisia guarantees free public higher education through a law rather than the constitution (Law No. 19-2008). The constitutions of Brazil, Finland, the Republic of Korea

and the Russian Federation guarantee access to higher education based on ability. (UNESCO, 2017, p 4)

UNESCO's report concludes (p 10) with six proposals for all university systems:

- clear equity targets;
- a legal framework;
- steering and monitoring agencies to enforce regulation;
- a level playing field for admission;
- tuition fees combined with means-tested loans and grants;
- limited student repayments.

Our suggestions draw on this framework, especially in the desire to rethink admissions and limit students' financial contribution. However, our proposals go beyond UNESCO's, in order to address challenges that we think will determine the future of higher education over the coming decades, including very rapid changes in the uses of technology and the nature of professional life, as well as growing inequalities. We argue that there should be a redistribution of higher education, in different proportions and at different stages of people's lives, across the whole adult population. Our hope is thus to think beyond a regulatory framework for 'access', since this continues to imply some policing of the borders of the university. In our system, equity would become a central pillar of the pedagogy and practice of institutions, a starting point rather than an afterthought.

In the remainder of this chapter, we consider the university system of our imagining in terms of structure, admissions, funding and participation.

Structure

1) A modular structure would replace degrees. The predominant existing degree structure would be abolished, with students instead taking modules and accumulating credits towards a range of possible outcomes.

2) There would be no point of graduation. The new, modular structure would have radical implications for admissions (discussed in Chapter 5), but would also mean abolishing the formal point of graduation. Instead, there would be an expectation that adults would continue to study and accumulate credits across the course of their lives, if they so wished.

3) There would be full participation. There would be a goal of full participation in further and higher education among those over 18, but this would come in a variety of modes and forms.

4) Part-time study would be the norm. Most students would work part-time and school-leavers would be encouraged to consider working full-time between school and university or to work alongside their studies.

5) University staff would also be university students. The student community would also include all staff members routinely studying while they worked (whether manual, technical, professional services or academic staff), while members of local and regional communities would join the university frequently at different points in their life.

6) Universities would work closely with employers. There would be much closer cooperation with employers of various kinds – including business, charities and industries – to provide continuing professional development, but also to create a culture of learning for its own sake in workplaces throughout the country.[2]

7) Higher, further, and community education providers would collaborate closely. Universities would work closely with further education colleges and other community education providers. Here, the focus would be on collaboration and cooperation, with universities learning just as much, if not more, from the partnerships – especially about how to provide accessible, relevant adult education.

8) The distinction between higher and further education would ultimately dissolve. As people move in and out of further and higher education throughout their lifetimes, they would be likely to access a mix of both academic and vocational education. This would lessen the distinction between these routes into and through higher education. Academic routes would no longer be the most prestigious option for young people; the narrow version of vocational education would not be seen as the only option for adult learners.

9) The distinction between Bachelor's and Master's study would dissolve. The distinction between undergraduate study (Bachelor's degrees, such as BAs, BScs and so on) and taught postgraduate study (Master's degrees, such as MAs, MScs and so on) will disappear. This distinction is already blurred in many programmes that allow students to upgrade from a BSc or BA to MSc or MA by studying for a further year within the undergraduate system. In the system we propose, Master's-level modules would be available alongside the other modules. They might come with prerequisites – a requirement to have studied certain previous modules in preparation – or they might not.

10) Admission to doctoral study would remain relatively unchanged. Currently, those wishing to study for a doctorate may cite a whole range of evidence: undergraduate and taught postgraduate achievements; relevant experience, such as that from their career so far, their involvement with various organisations, or their previous creative output, if relevant; and a research proposal, which is often crafted in collaboration with the potential supervisor. As part-time undergraduate study becomes the norm, we would also anticipate that PhDs might be studied part-time over four to six years, with more coherent support for those studying in this mode. This would help ease some of the anxieties and mental health barriers that arise from the isolating and highly pressured experience, at least in arts and humanities and the social sciences, of studying as a lone scholar for such an extended period.

11) Doctoral study would be treated as a job. As in the Dutch system, researching for a PhD would be considered a job, and students would be paid a salary (full- or part-time) by the university to undertake it. Alongside the academic research required by this job, PhD students would undertake undergraduate teaching (as in the US Graduate Teaching Assistantship schemes) and community engagement work. This would embed them in their home department, and would also provide them with crucial professional training should they go on to pursue an academic career.

Admissions

12) Access to initial study would be completely open. All those physically present in a country, including refugees and asylum seekers, would be able to access up to 60 credits of study in further/higher education on an open access basis and for free.

13) Access to some routes beyond initial study would be completely open. Beyond 60 credits, there would be a variety of routes through subsequent study for which no additional prior qualifications would be required.

14) Access to specialist routes beyond initial study would be fairer. There would continue to be a limited number of 'specialist' routes through subsequent study, for example where a particular route might be required for a profession. Entry to these routes would be on the basis of two of the following conditions: achievement in the prior 60 credits; achievement in a prior course of study; interview and/or written work set at the point of admission.

15) Admissions would treat state education as the norm. Where achievement in prior study is considered at the point of admission, there would be a standard offer – for example, for the 93% of students attending state schools, or for those taking an Access course – and then a higher offer for students attending a private school.

16) University admissions would be decoupled from school results. The proposed changes to admissions would largely decouple university admissions from achievement in the school system, and align higher education much more closely with the further education sector, with the aim of ultimately dissolving the distinction between the two. The implications for schools are potentially very positive. Freed from the pressure to become 'exam factories', they would be able to turn their attention away from testing and develop more creative approaches to education.

17) Applications to doctoral study from those without prior university qualifications would be supported. As already happens in many disciplines in the current system, students would be able to commence doctoral study without having completed a prior programme of study. Relevant vocational or other experience would be considered as equivalent to prior academic experience, and short preparatory courses for doctoral study would be developed to support candidates entering the academy at this stage. Employers would support their staff to pursue this route, and might co-design the proposal, where the doctorate would have direct relevance to a project or dilemma in the workplace.

Funding

18) Initial study would be free for all. The first 60 credits of study would be free as well as open access. This entitlement would be for 60 successful credits and all learners would also be entitled to up to 40 unsuccessful credits, to allow for modules where an individual might (for example) opt not to take the assessment or fail on the first attempt. We estimate that this would cost approximately £5 billion.[3]

19) Lifelong learning would become the norm. Students would be able to accumulate as many credits as they wish over the course of their lives, at a variety of levels.

20) University teaching would be funded by a participatory education tax. The fees and loans system would be replaced with an all-age graduate tax, called a participatory education tax (PET). It would be paid by all past graduates and all those who, in future, accumulated more than 60 credits. An individual would pay a slightly higher rate of tax after accumulating 240 credits of study. See Box 1.1 for details.

Box 1.1: How would the participatory education tax work?

As Green and Mason (2017) have shown, an 'all-age' graduate tax – applied to past undergraduates as well – would be more equitable and sustainable than the existing fees system in the UK, which puts all of the cost on to current and future 'graduates' and in which high levels of non-repayment are increasingly predicted. Green and Mason suggest this model would create higher revenues for government than at present, but more equitable repayments. They estimate that in their model a student would make the same repayments they owe in the current system (when earning over £21,000) only once they are earning £60,000. We propose a slightly amended version of Green and Mason's second option, as follows, and would rename it a participatory education tax (PET):

- For people who have accumulated between 60 and 240 credits:
  a. 0.5% added to the Basic Rate of income tax;
  b. 1.5% added to the Higher Rate of income tax.
- For those who have accumulated 240 credits and upwards:
  c. 1.0% added to the Basic Rate;
  d. 2.0% added to the Higher Rate.

We propose that the taxation continues into retirement, whereas Green and Mason propose that the tax is levied only from the age of 20-64. We estimate that this would raise at least £2.6 billion in annual revenue based on the *current* number of graduates in the UK who received subsidised education, which is considerably more than the £1.8 billion raised during 2015-16 by repayments through the student loans system.[4]

Those who took out full-fee student loans during the lifetime of that scheme would be exempt from the PET. However, they would be able to opt in to the tax scheme if they wished. If they did this, the outstanding debt on their student loan would be cancelled. Moreover, any previous payments that they had made towards that debt would be deducted from their PET taxation liability.

Of course, if our proposals generate the higher levels of participation intended, the number of those who fall within the 'all-age' PET tax will increase. Consider the following future situation:

- 90% of the 18-and-above population are participating;
- 10% of those participating have accumulated up to 60 credits, 30% have accumulated 60-240 credits, and 60% have accumulated more than 240 credits;
- the division of the population into tax bands is the same as we have now (that is, approximately 80% on Basic Rate only, approximately 15% also on Higher Rate);
- the mean income for those participating is lower than the mean income for graduates now, since there are so many more participating – let's say £26,000 mean for those on Basic Rate, and £48,000 for those also on Higher Rate.

In this situation, the PET tax will generate around £18.4 billion.

If we assume that those who accumulate 60 to 240 credits accumulate a mean of 180 credits at a cost of £75 each over 60 years, while those who accumulate 240 credits and above accumulate a mean of 360 credits at a cost of £75 each over 60 years, the cost of higher education will be around £18.1 billion per year.[5]

21) Half of PET revenue would be allocated centrally for strategic purposes. Of the funding provided via the PET tax, 50% would be distributed through a national system, which would allow, for example, for the identification of strategic priorities across the sector, including in response to global challenges and research priorities emerging internationally. We assume here that this would continue to be on a devolved basis, with England, Northern Ireland, Scotland and Wales each maintaining a separate system for higher education (and, indeed, choosing whether or not to move to this model of funding).

22) Half of the PET revenue would be distributed in each region through a system of participatory budgeting. The other 50% of funding raised would be distributed through an annual participatory budgeting process in each region, furthering the process of devolution. This participatory budgeting process – modelled on examples such as the longstanding arrangements for civic participatory budgeting in Porto Alegre in Brazil (see Marquetti et al, 2012) – would begin with a series of public meetings or plenaries, in which the previous year would be reviewed and critiqued. This would also allow for a wide range of opinions to be heard on what the priorities should be, in teaching and research, over the coming year. Plenary participants would then elect delegates to participate in local forums, and finally to a regional forum, in which the final budget would be decided. This participatory budgeting model would be designed to ensure universities are accountable to communities and that those communities feel ownership of the knowledge that is produced in them.

Box 1.2: Would a participatory budgeting model work?

A participatory budgeting process creates the possibility of much greater democratic participation and accountability than in the present system. However, there is some evidence that participatory budgeting models can reproduce existing hierarchies within communities, with dominant or established voices better able to influence the system (see Wainwright [2003] as well as Marquetti et al [2012]). A well-funded charity might be able to shape proposals more easily than a group of marginalised individuals with common interests but little capacity to organise themselves. But while a participatory budgeting model might initially reproduce some of the existing power structures, it would give participants the tools they need to remake the system for themselves on an ongoing basis. Universities are a particularly appropriate structure to fund on this basis: Marquetti and colleagues emphasise the 'pedagogical effect' of such a model on participants (2012, p 63). All those physically present in a region might contribute, so the voices of those often excluded from civic decision making – such as refugees and asylum seekers and those in prison – could be heard. This would also ensure that the experiences of those arriving from some of the world's most challenging environments would inform the priorities set; participation at a local level could thus help shape the search for curricular justice on a global scale. We suggest a 50-50 split between a national and regional funding model. This would ensure that universities focused on national and global challenges, as well as local ones, and mitigate the risk that large inequalities might develop in the quality of teaching and research in different regions.

---

23) Regions would have the power to raise additional funds for higher education. This participatory budgeting would, in the first instance, be on the basis of the funding allocated from an all-age learner contribution tax, but each region would also have discretionary powers to raise taxes, if agreed in the regional forum, in order to fund an expansion of specific activities – say, the provision of more courses on a particular topic, or to fund research in a particular area.

24) Universities would become more responsive to societal needs. This form of participatory budgeting would ensure that all universities work much more closely with society on the challenges of the coming decades, including climate change, technology and the disruptions it will cause to existing patterns of life – including through growing inequality, movement of people, and the challenges of governance in a changing society. Such participation is vital for pragmatic as well as idealistic reasons. Universities cannot understand the nature of these challenges if they reproduce the exclusions that are at the heart of each of them.

Participation

25) Local communities would have priority in initial study. There would be an emphasis on participation by those in the local area and region adjacent to each university, especially for the first 60 credits of study. All institutions would give priority in admissions to individuals for whom they are the nearest college or university.

26) Dedicated student housing would be integrated with other housing models. There would be options to move away from home for your studies, especially after 60 credits. However, the model in which students live in segregated housing would be diluted by an emphasis on part-time study, with much more shared student and social housing and with opportunities for students to undertake paid or voluntary work within their residences, for example in shared accommodation with vulnerable young people or retirement housing. This would build on imaginative models that are developing throughout the UK designed to create shared intergenerational living spaces.

27) Childcare would be central to all universities. Adrienne Rich's (1979) proposals for childcare would be at the centre of all institutions:

> Childcare would be available for all students, staff, and faculty, with additional places for community children, at a subsidized rate that would make it effectively open to all. This is an absolute necessary, though not sufficient, condition for the kinds of change we envision. Childcare would be of the highest quality ... (p 148)

28) Flexible learning and assessment would become the norm. All learning and assessment would be as flexible and inclusive as possible, so that students would always have an opportunity to study in a mode appropriate to their learning style. Universities would operate on a model – drawing on the potential of digital technologies – that would ensure those with disabilities and/or learning difficulties could be included wherever possible and with modes of learning and assessment appropriate to their needs already provided, so they would not have to declare a disability or wait for adjustments to be made. This would require the development of user-friendly digital technologies, helping to close the 'digital divide' with those who currently have little or no access to the online world or literacy in its use.

29) All curricula would be inclusive. The structure of all curricula would actively encourage students to bring their existing life experience and knowledge into the classroom, and to share what they are learning with others as part of their studies.

30) Communities would be involved in setting priorities. The participatory budgeting model would allow communities in the region to be involved in setting the teaching and research priorities of institutions, ensuring that universities would also increasingly recognise alternative knowledges and ways of knowing.

31) The history of exclusion from universities would form part of curricula on all courses. At the start of their studies within universities, all students would learn about histories of the university, including the exclusion of women, people from ethnic minorities, those with disabilities, and those from working-class communities, lower income households and other disadvantaged communities. This would model a way of teaching that acknowledges, for example, colonialism and racism – and would feed into ensuring that subsequent discussions are also informed by awareness of those voices that may still be missing or underrepresented and an ongoing need to work towards greater equality.

32) Distinctive communities of knowledge would be created. Within the participatory budgeting model, local communities would be encouraged to explore options to create (for example) female, working-class, and Black, Asian and minority ethnic communities of knowledge that would still be in dialogue with the larger university structure, but provide opportunities to decentre the university away from the white, male patriarchal – and hierarchical – model that has dominated it so far. These communities of knowledge would come in a variety of forms, including colleges or faculties, but also smaller and informal groupings that would receive financial support and institutional recognition.

33) Communities of knowledge would be responsive to changes in society. It would be vital that these structures could be reconstituted or reformed, as new ideas and relationships develop. This more responsive university structure would be designed to reflect the way in which some radical interventions *are* temporary – including if they achieve their aims – and also that structures themselves need to be constantly tested and reworked.

2

Invisible crises: the state of universities in the UK

Imagine if this morning you had read the following news article:

> The number of people choosing to study as an undergraduate at university in England has plummeted by 61% in the past seven years, according to a study published on Wednesday. The report, which was commissioned by ministers, says that reasons for the drop include a tough economic climate, but suggests that the government's decision to triple tuition fees to a maximum of £9,000 has played a decisive part. The report found that those now less likely to attend come from groups that are already underrepresented in higher education.

A 61% drop in student numbers. A clear link to a new funding regime that the government had introduced. A particularly bad effect on the most vulnerable groups in society. Surely, if you read such a report, it would signal a crisis. It is likely that some universities would be closing, or would face a severe financial crisis. Ministers might resign; a rethink would be imminent. Would this even be enough to bring down a government?

This article is not entirely fictional, although it is unlikely that you would have heard it as headline news. There is one word missing: the number of people choosing to study *part-time* at university in England has dropped by 61% since 2010. These changes tend to be discussed (if at all) as a side issue: in the media, by government ministers, and within universities. The decline in part-time undergraduates is seen as a regrettable by-product of a system that is nonetheless recruiting more students than ever before, including those from backgrounds that are not well represented in higher education. One reason part-time students have been invisible is because they do not apply for their programmes through the national Universities and Colleges Admissions Service (UCAS). As a consequence, figures for full-time students who have applied through that route are routinely quoted as if they represent the whole student population.

What happens if we count full- and part-time students together? According to Universities UK (2017), in 2011/12 there were 2,105,730 undergraduate students in universities and further education colleges, once all modes of study are included. There were 173,390 fewer students by 2015/16, a fall of about 8% (Universities UK, 2017, p 11). In other words: the overall number of students in the system has fallen. Peter Horrocks (2017), vice-chancellor of the Open University (OU) until 2018, has suggested that disadvantaged students have been particularly affected. He showed that while there has been a 7% rise in disadvantaged students going to university full-time since 2012, the number of part-time students from the same areas has nearly halved. As a consequence, the overall number of students from disadvantaged backgrounds entering universities in England has dropped 15% since 2011. (See also Callender and Thompson [2018, p 4] for detailed figures on who has been affected by the changes.)

Part-time students are overwhelmingly 'mature', which in the UK is defined as over the age of 21. They are more likely to be women, to be from a minority ethnic background, to have a disability, or to have caring responsibilities. They are much less likely to have followed a conventional route through school. As Adrienne Rich (1979) notes: 'The notion of the full-time student has penalized both women and the poor' (p 150). The decline in part-time study has further accelerated regional inequalities in terms of who accesses higher education in England. A report from the former Higher Education Funding Council for England (HEFCE, 2014b) showed that between 2011 and 2012, for example, the decline in part-time undergraduate entrants was nearly twice as fast in the north-east as in the south-east of England. The sharpest drops were in the north-east, north-west and in Yorkshire and Humberside (p 20). Part-time students also often wish to study in small chunks over a longer period of time, rather than enrolling for a whole degree. Yet, since 2012, there has been an overwhelming emphasis on degree-length qualifications, at the expense of shorter learning opportunities, including many short courses on which students were supported in the past by employers.

The situation has worsened as reduced demand has also led to fewer part-time courses. A university has not yet closed because of the decline in part-time study, but centres and institutes focused on lifelong learning have shut their doors steadily over the past two decades, in response to repeated funding changes and cuts (Jones et al, 2010). There is overwhelming evidence that the whole system is becoming more uniform and that the student population is now increasingly homogenous. The impact of the post-2012 changes on Birkbeck in London and the OU, two universities that have catered particularly to part-time students, has been profound. Birkbeck is London's 'evening university', and in 2010, part-time students made up nearly all of its undergraduate population. By 2015, it had more full-time than part-time students (UK Parliament, House of Commons, 2018). The effect on other institutions in the sector that were traditionally geared towards part-time study has been equally serious, and controversial changes are now being implemented at the OU (Wilby, 2018).

It is clear that some part-time students have chosen to walk away from the current system, and that the change in the financial system has been a factor in those decisions. When the new funding system was introduced from 2012/13, it was supposed to level the playing field between full- and part-time students, bringing part-time students into the system of loans and repayments from which they had been excluded since 1997. Yet Claire Callender (2017) notes: 'The terms and conditions are unattractive to those who are eligible for the loans. The government anticipated that a third of part-time students would take one out, but only a fifth have done so.'

So why have some part-time students voted with their feet? Let's take the example of Sumita, a 35-year-old, working-class single parent with two children, who works in a full-time job where she currently earns £550 per week or £28,600 per year, which is the average salary in the UK (ONS, 2017). It would always have been challenging for Sumita to re-enter education as an adult, and there might have been financial risks under any system. Yet the current system does little to mitigate the risks. If she started an undergraduate degree in 2017 and took out a loan for tuition, Sumita would (at today's prices) start paying back £57 per month from the fourth year of her studies in 2021 (or 9% of her earnings above the threshold of £21,000). There would thus be a drop in her income, of £684 per annum – slightly more than one week's wages – in year five and six of her degree, if she remained in the same job and at the same salary (without factoring in inflation or the interest on her loan).

Let's assume that Sumita graduates and, because of her degree, enters a profession that pays a higher salary of £32,000. She would then, at current prices, start paying back around £83 per month, or £990 per year. A single parent in this situation might well already have existing debts, such as a mortgage, or be managing rising costs such as rent or the need to have a deposit available for new accommodation because of insecure housing. Sumita might also wish to save money to support her children in entering higher education. All of this is without factoring in the potential loss of earnings Sumita might experience if she works fewer hours while studying or needs to arrange additional childcare for the times she attends classes. In 2018/19, maintenance loans will be introduced for part-time students in England but, until now, students have had to fund their living costs while studying themselves.

The choices Sumita would have to make are not straightforward and it is possible that, on balance, she might still choose to undertake a degree. But it is easy to see why a marginal gain in income in the long term might seem to have little to recommend it when set against the costs in the short and medium term. It is also clear that it is Sumita herself who bears responsibility for the risks, a stressful situation for someone whose life situation allows limited margin for error. It is also clear that a prolonged degree carries much greater risks of her not completing her course than a short programme of study: life could intervene in many unexpected ways across a six-year course.

In relative terms, Sumita is comfortable financially. Imagine a different student, Annette, who is a single parent with one child. Annette works as a nursery nurse and earns £12,000 per year, and grew up in a family with debts and whose family home was repossessed when she was nine. For a student like Annette, a potential debt of more than twice her annual earnings, for tuition alone, is an enormous disincentive to studying, even though she would not start to repay anything until her income nearly doubles. That distinction has proved too abstract for many, and especially those who have already experienced debt as a damaging force in their life (see Callender and Mason, 2017).

One of the questions now facing universities in the UK is whether part-time study is an exceptional case, or whether the fate of part-time students is a sign that the system that may not be sustainable in the long term. What if similar consequences play out across the lives of younger students who are currently graduating with high levels of debt? What if such students cannot find the rewarding work (financially and otherwise) that a degree was supposed to give them? What if they defer major life choices, such as marriage or buying a home, because of the debt? What if a message gradually works its way through the system that it isn't worth going to university?

These questions are not entirely hypothetical. Applications to UK universities by full-time home students fell by 4% in 2017, with drops in all regions of the country (UCAS, 2017). A report by the Chartered Institute of Personnel and Development notes that 58.8% of graduates in the UK are in jobs deemed to be non-graduate roles, a percentage exceeded only in Greece and Estonia (CIPD, 2015). The consequences are especially acute for working-class students and those from particular ethnic minorities. Diane Reay (2017) has argued that class inequalities have 'shifted from being primarily about exclusion from the system to being about exclusion within it' (p 118), a significant finding for the full-time sector, albeit one that misses how the decline in part-time opportunities is creating new exclusions from the system itself. Reay shows that full-time students from lower income backgrounds graduate with on average £14,000 more debt than their peers and that working-class students on a 'special-entry' scheme at a Russell Group university were significantly less likely to get a graduate job than their middle- and upper-class peers (p 128). The issues about exclusion within the system are also acute for Black, Asian and minority ethnic students, with Black students more than twice as likely to drop out of their degrees than White students in 2014/15 and fewer than half of Black students achieving a first-class or upper second-class degree, compared with nearly 70% of their White peers (OFFA, 'Topic briefing: BME students', undated).

There is evidence that the current system is adding to the pressures already faced by young people. They are dealing with an unwelcome mix of economic insecurity, high levels of debt and unprecedented levels of anxiety, not helped by the pressures created in an examination-focused school system and the intense scrutiny (and self-scrutiny) created by social media. In a survey in 2015 by the National Union of Students (NUS, 2016), three out of four students said they had experienced mental health issues during the previous years, while a third said they had had suicidal thoughts. Among those who did not identify as heterosexual, the latter figure was 55%. A recent report by the Institute of Public Policy Research (IPPR, 2017) found that 15,395 UK-domiciled first-year students disclosed a mental health condition in 2015/16, almost five times the number in 2006/07. The rhetoric about tuition fees, when they were introduced and increased, suggested they would empower students to shape and influence the course of their education. These figures suggest a very different experience.

★

Much of what we have discussed so far in this chapter might be framed as the (perhaps) unintended consequences of a mass higher education system. In the early 2000s, the then prime minister Tony Blair committed the New Labour government to achieving a target of half of young people progressing to university. The focus on young people was one driver for the decline in older students: the target created momentum for subsequent funding changes, as the government tried to meet its headline figure. Yet the target itself shifted, almost imperceptibly. It was initially for 50% of 18- 30-year-olds to have some experience of higher education (Taylor, 2009, p 80); it quickly became half of school-leavers instead. Concerns were expressed at the time about the fact that the 50% target was arbitrary, leading to 'more of the same' groups attending (Taylor, 2009, p 74). One consequence has been an uneven distribution of who attends: some groups and communities are participating more, while others are participating only a little more or hardly at all.

One of the reasons why recruitment to full-time courses at universities has remained relatively consistent may be that the opportunities outside the system have been diminishing at speed. The increase in university places has taken place alongside a drastic reduction in opportunities in further education. The adult skills budget was cut by 40% between 2010 and 2016 (Robertson, 2017). At the same time, skills in the young adult population are declining. The Organisation for Economic Co-operation and Development (OECD, 2017) found in a survey of 34 countries that the UK has one of the highest rates of literacy and numeracy in the 55-64 age group, but is in the bottom 10 for 16- to 24-year-olds. If it is a difficult time to be within the university system, the pressures outside of it are significantly greater.

The relationship between universities and the public realm is also changing, as a consequence of the funding model, with implications for how students view themselves and their institutions. David Watson (2009) argued that, 'When Vice-Chancellors are asked whether their institutions are in the public or the private sector, the correct answer is "yes"' (p 17). In the decade since Watson's comment, the balance has shifted towards the private sector. One rationale for higher student fees was that those who benefit should also be the ones who pay. This narrow view of the benefits of higher education is understandable, but it is also divisive. There have been numerous flashpoints recently between universities, some of which are expanding, and cities that are facing the realities of austerity cuts in public services and for whom studentification (the process by which an area takes on housing, services and other characteristics driven by student needs) is a mixed blessing. In autumn 2017, the University of Bristol announced a plan for a new £80 million library, at a time when 17 of Bristol's 27 public libraries faced closure, drawing this response from Eleanor Combley, a Green Party councillor:

Our universities bring many benefits to us as a city. However, current government policy forces universities to grow or die. This unlimited growth places strains on city services, whilst their tax exempt status and the loss of the central government grant which used to compensate us for students' council tax exemption means they don't really pay their way. It boggles the mind to consider that the university is able to spend on one library a sum that would allow Bristol City Council to keep all our libraries open for 50 years. And to me, it underlines the point that there is money in the economy and that the impoverishment of our public services is a political choice. (Booth, 2017)

Combley articulates a clear risk to the university system: that it will lose public trust, and be seen as increasingly well resourced and remote by those outside of it who do not share the benefits. East Palo Alto, discussed in the Introduction, may give us a glimpse how university towns in the UK might develop, if inequalities accelerate in the 2020s, in an economy oriented even further towards digital technology and automation. There are precedents for universities nurturing and depending on local libraries, as the OU did when it was founded. Lizzie Brown's story also shows how vital libraries can be as part of what Adrienne Rich calls an 'unofficial university-without-walls'. But there would be risks to an institution opening its library to the public in the current funding model, in which students want to know they are seeing the benefits of their own significant financial investment.

Divisions are opening up between different geographical areas of England, as well as within them. In late 2017, it was reported that for the first time in 110 years, life expectancy in the UK is no longer rising (Dorling and Gietel-Basten, 2018). Within the figures (ONS, 2015), there are enormous geographic disparities between life expectancy in the wealthiest areas of the south and east of England, and parts of northern England

and the regions, where it is falling. The ONS report speculates that the increasing disparities in life expectancy may also be a consequence of certain kinds of social and geographic mobility:

> It is also possible that there is a selective migration of healthy individuals from deprived areas in other regions into London for employment or other economic reasons. This type of migration has been shown to raise ill-health and death rates where these people originated from and lower them where they moved to. (ONS, 2015, p 7)

There are many factors that can lead to 'selective migration'. But the UK higher education system is one of them: it encourages social and geographic mobility for a relatively small percentage of the population. Donnelly and Gamsu (2018) show that: 'Staying at home and studying locally is strongly differentiated by ethnicity and social background with students from disadvantaged groups much more likely to be living at home' (p 4). Those who are mobile are also less likely to return home after graduation to regions where employment prospects are narrower. As Donnelly and Gamsu argue:

> A more sustainable regional economic policy would seek to place universities with large numbers of local commuter students, who are far more likely to stay local on graduation, at the centre of regional development. For those who do move away from marginalised communities, policymakers should consider how they can be provided with employment opportunities in their home areas which are of similar quality to those that can be found elsewhere. This would require a structural approach which sees higher education, access and spatial and social mobility as one element in the transformation of the unequal regional economies of the UK. (p 26)

★

The proposals we outlined in Chapter 1 take inspiration from wider models of adult education, in the UK and elsewhere. They would make universities more responsive to the population in their local area as well as to the varied shape of individual lives, to which further education colleges have often responded more readily. Some of the potential objections to this shift are easily stated. It might be argued that students without A-Levels, or any conventional qualifications, will not be prepared for university study or that an increase in the number of students entering higher education is likely to reduce the quality (of the students admitted or the teaching offered). It could be argued, as Wendy Piatt implies in the statement from the Russell Group quoted in the Introduction, that what is really needed is reform of the school system or additional funding for early years' education in particular. Objections might equally be raised from within the adult education sector: why turn universities into a version of adult education, rather than funding further education itself better and giving it greater prestige? There might well be scepticism about whether these reforms would really enable such a broad range of people to enter higher education, or would simply be an expensive way of rearranging provision for those who already attend. From another perspective, one could argue that the ideas we are putting forward make universities primarily local institutions, at a time when they need to be thinking of themselves as international.

It may sound utopian to change the basis of the admissions system. But until 1945, entry to university only required six passes at GCE level (Blackman, 2015) while, since 1969, the OU has shown that a 'comprehensive'-style higher education system, which is open to all regardless of prior qualifications, is feasible. There would be some limits. There may be some adults with cognitive disabilities, for whom higher education is not the most appropriate learning environment. Yet there is an opportunity to create radically different modes of participation in higher education, including through digital resources, that could open universities to a much broader range of students, including those with a range of disabilities. This would build on the transformative work of the OU which, in its early years, had a dramatic impact on those facing mobility challenges, who were able to access a distance education from wherever they were living. We explore these questions about admissions at greater length in Chapter 5.

More broadly, this model acknowledges that not everyone wishes to participate in formal education, of any kind. After all, the first right anyone has in such a system is the right to *not* participate. In the university system we imagine, this right would be central. But because individuals would increasingly opt out rather than in, non-participation would be an informed choice, and one that could be revoked at any time. In the current system, it is too often a choice made by someone else (a parent, teacher, or careers adviser) or by a prospective student on the basis of a feeling of not being good enough or fear of not fitting in, out of ignorance about the options available, or due to accidents of circumstance. And, once a student has chosen not to go to university at 18, their options narrow and the contextual disincentives against returning to education increase rapidly.

The tensions between being a global and local institution are overstated. As we have seen, and will explore further in later chapters, the model we propose is intrinsically international, albeit in different ways and for (partially) different ends than the current system. International students often come to the UK for a year, a semester, or a fraction of their course, so that this model would still work well for those studying in that mode. A credit system (properly realised) would make moving between UK and international institutions easier rather than more difficult. And, while full-time study would no longer be the 'norm' from which part-time students 'deviate', full-time study would remain an option.

Some of the arguments against this model have been made before. The setting up of the OU met with a chorus of scepticism. 'How can the ideas of open access and evaluative exit be reconciled?' asked the journal *Education*, with barely concealed doubts about whether those without conventional prior qualifications would achieve success at the end of a degree. Stuart Hood, former controller of the BBC television service, wrote that it was: 'The most expensive method of inefficient further education ever conceived.' He predicted that drop-out rates would be high. Many were sceptical about who could be reached, and whether they needed a degree at all. The *New Statesman* was not alone in asking: 'How many [of the proposed students] would be house bound women? Do they want degrees? Would they make any real use of the degree style courses and, if they did, qualify?' (all cited in Hollis, 1998, pp 308, 311).

The OU is not a perfect institution, of course, and critiques have been made of its limitations. But there is no denying that it was ahead of its time, pioneering distance learning decades before the internet. We need a similar moment of anticipation, to remake higher education for the next hundred years (or more). Here is what Jim, in the ranks of the Royal Air Force, wrote in the OU's magazine, *Sesame*, in 1979, in an article on the first 10 years of the university:

By the time I had completed A100 it had pushed and guided me into gathering up great quantities of clutter in my mind and throwing it out for ever.... Through the Reformation, via Calvin and Knox I found the meaning of my childhood socialisation, and through Kant a moral philosopher that is now an essential part of my everyday criteria. War and Society gave deeper meaning to my RAF days and to my post-war experience of the misery and destitution I had seen among the rubble and desolation of the German cities. It linked with the multitudinous beggary I had tried to ignore in India and it interrelated

with my A401 research into pauperism in mid-Victorian
England and what I had seen of the Depression in the early
Thirties. Essentially the OU brought cause to what I had
experienced only as effect. (Cited in Hollis, 1998, p 350)

It is not hard to think of other areas where a study of causes might
lead to a useful conversation about effects. The campaigner
Doreen Lawrence has long argued that if a wider cross-section
of the population understood the effects of colonialism and its
impact on migration to the UK, there would be a very different
understanding of race in Britain (Adams, 2013). The very fact of
engaging in education itself has been shown to have beneficial
effects: Schuller and colleagues (2004) found that those engaging
in adult learning of any kind were more likely to give up
smoking, engage in exercise and increase their life satisfaction,
but also to be increasingly racially tolerant, less politically cynical
and have heightened political interests (pp 167-8).

The benefits work both ways. Jim suggests he was throwing
out 'clutter' in his mind, but it is clear that he brought a wide
range of experiences to his studies of war, poverty and society.
There would be benefits to universities in a system that included
more students like him. It would allow universities to understand
the effects of ideas that are often studied within their walls as
abstract causes. Indeed, this argument was central to the extra-
mural tradition within which E.P. Thompson, Stuart Hall and
Raymond Williams worked throughout their careers. It is this
tradition that Thompson was defending when he suggested
the need to test education continually against a range of life
experience. Thompson noted that democracy would realise itself
('if it does') in 'our *whole* society' and that 'for this to happen, the
universities need the abrasion of different worlds of experience,
in which ideas are brought to the test of life' (1997, p 30).

Recent political events in the UK have powerfully
demonstrated how divisive different 'worlds of experience' can
prove to be. The emerging political landscape exposed by the

EU membership referendum (or Brexit) vote in 2016 and the 2017 general election is complex. Yet, in both votes, two sides emerged that were incomprehensible to each other and they split, above all, along levels of education. David Runciman (2016) wrote of the Brexit vote: 'Voters with postgraduate qualifications split 75 to 25 in favour of remain. Meanwhile, among those who left school without any qualifications, the vote was almost exactly reversed: 73 to 27 for leave.' He concluded: 'Class still matters. Age still matters. But education appears to matter more.' The figures are similarly instructive for the US presidential election in 2016 (Silver, 2016). This is not to imply that increased participation in higher education would help people to vote the 'right' way. Rather, these figures highlight that we are witnessing a crisis in what forms of knowledge we hold in common as a society, with too little dialogue between expertise and experience. Reform of our universities is an important step in addressing this, as we explore at greater length in Chapter 6.

Another objection might be that we are better off without universities altogether, that some of the most transformative educational experiences happen outside them. We do not deny this. Recent attempts to reimagine the forms of higher education elsewhere have included the Social Science Centre in Lincoln and the burgeoning cooperative university movement (Neary and Amsler, 2012). There is also evidence that the private sector may innovate in ways that the existing system has not: the New Model in Technology and Engineering project, a 'new model of high-value engineering education', to be based in Hereford, is one example, although at present its admissions model is surprisingly conservative.[6]

Adrienne Rich (1979) writes that real social change is likely to come from outside universities and that it is 'probable' that 'the unrecognized, unofficial university-without-walls ... will prove a far more important agent in reshaping the foundations on which human life is now organized' (p 127). Yet she concedes:

The orthodox university is still a vital spot ... if only because it is a place where people can find each other and begin to hear each other. (It is also a source of certain kinds of power.) (1979, p 127)

Education has a vital democratic function, not least in providing spaces where individuals from dramatically different backgrounds can meet – at times, on equal terms. This is true in particular ways in universities, where the knowledge that is created has a key role in determining the future of wider society; those with a stake in its creation thus shape the ideas and priorities that result. At a time of rising inequalities and growing social divisions, universities remain vital if – as a society – we are to begin to hear one another again.

3

'It's not for me': outsiders in the system

For more than 10 years, I had an office on the first floor of the University of Bristol English Department, which is located in a large 19th-century villa on a road in Clifton, the wealthiest suburb of the city. The front entrance to the building is a more recent glass structure that sits between two older buildings. Throughout the day, staff, students and visitors come and go – and on the hour, as lectures or seminars start and end, large waves of people pass by. There is a desk, where the porters who are on duty sit, but there is no formal reception area.

There was one student who, no matter how often she came to see me, would never just turn up and knock on my office door. Instead, Nina would wait for a porter, and then ask them to ring up and tell me she had arrived. She was the only student I knew who did this, and I found it such a baffling ritual that I did not say anything for a long time. In the fourth year of her degree, Nina was around 15 minutes late for a meeting with me, because there had not been a porter on duty when she arrived. In exasperation, I said: "You don't need to wait – you can just come and knock on my door."

Several years later, I asked Nina to speak on a panel about black and minority ethnic (BME) experience at the university.

The university's Students' Union had recently published a report on this topic (Bristol SU, 2016), which found that students often felt isolated 'due to being the only, or one of a few, BME students in a room' and that 'many students reported feeling that they couldn't be "completely themselves"' (p 15). Students also reported experiences of direct racism and racist micro-aggressions and the survey raised concerns about mental health.

Nina talked about her educational history at the event, some of which I had heard before. She is in her forties and left school without qualifications, in part due to dyslexia, which was only diagnosed in her thirties. She spent years being late, she said, because she had to ask other people for the time, as she could not read a clock. In 2009, Nina had taken a short taster course that the university had developed with the local Black Development Agency, on Black life writing. She recalled being transfixed by the woman who taught the course, because she had never seen a Black teacher before. Nina subsequently took another short course at the university. After some hesitation, she applied for the BA in English Literature and Community Engagement, a six-year course that is taught one night per week. We designed this programme to be accessible to those who might not have expected to be at university a year, or even six months, beforehand – and Nina's journey into the university had been unexpected and rapid.

Nina told another story at the event. She recalled the same occasion on which I told her that she didn't need to wait, and that she should just come and knock on my door when she arrived. Nina said that this conversation had made her realise that she still felt like an outsider in the university, even after four years of study: she was still asking for permission to enter, and expecting to be told to leave. In Thomas Hardy's novel, *Jude the Obscure*, the eponymous hero arrives in the fictional university town of Christminster, where he has longed to become a student:

It was not till now, when he found himself actually on the spot of his enthusiasm, that Jude perceived how far away from the object of that enthusiasm he really was. Only a wall divided him from those happy young contemporaries of his with whom he shared a common mental life; men who had nothing to do from morning till night but to read, mark, learn, and inwardly digest. Only a wall – but what a wall! (2016, p 72)

The borders of a university are not always marked in this way and there have been attempts, since the late 19th century, to navigate around the boundaries: 'extra-mural' departments were those that offered courses outside the university walls. But borders exist – often invisible ones – and they can be difficult to cross, as Nina's story makes clear. She is a lifelong Bristol resident, who lives barely a mile from campus, for whom the White and privileged space of campus is alienating. Even once (and especially when) she was inside the university, Nina felt like an outsider.

Nina's longer story is also about educational institutions more widely: she also had negative experiences in school and college. Diane Reay (2017) quotes the experiences of Josie, a White, working-class single mother whom Reay interviewed about her experiences of supporting her two sons through their education. Josie describes an episode from her own schooling, when she was seven, in which she was sent out of the room for asking too many questions about a topic she did not understand. Another student was sent out to tell Josie that she could come back in if she 'apologised'. Josie did not know what this word meant:

If I'd have known what it meant…. I was just too embarrassed to go in. I was only seven and it was a class of 35 children and she'd be standing there saying 'Come on, apologise' and me not knowing what apologise meant. I daren't go in. So it was a whole lot of misunderstanding. (Reay, 2017, p 68)

The story encapsulates a number of ways in which exclusion can occur. A student is sent outside of the classroom because their lack of understanding cannot be contained within the situation or perhaps because their questions are also challenging for the teacher. She is then doubly excluded, both by her lack of understanding (or excess of it) and by an inability to navigate the social and linguistic codes that would allow her to re-enter the educational space.

This chapter explores why we need to change the system itself, rather than just 'admitting' different people to it. In her essay 'Towards a woman-centred university', Adrienne Rich (1979) reminds us that universities were designed to educate (wealthy, White) young men. She quotes a bulletin from Brandeis University in the United States that claims it has 'set itself to develop the whole man'. Rich remarks: 'This is no semantic game or trivial accident of language. What we have at present *is* a man-centred university, a breeding ground not of humanism, but of masculine privilege' (1979, p 127). Rich highlights the extent to which universities have been structured around an act of exclusion (of women), and that even once inside those universities, women still contend with structures that have been designed to educate men. Rich also shows how such structural exclusions are both constructed and reproduced in language.

For a year in 2015-16, I worked with a charity in Bristol that supports people who have been out of society – whether in prison, through experiences of addiction or homelessness, because of mental health issues or for another reason – by providing them with education and training that gives them new skills. I once asked a volunteer, Debbie, who had herself come through the training programme, what anxieties participants most frequently had about education. Debbie said that if she went into any institutional space there would be a language barrier and she would feel excluded *before* a conversation started. She cited, as examples, a benefits office, a college, a university, an employer and a recruitment company. A single word could be enough to make her feel self-conscious and as if she could not cope. She said this was common to most of the participants in the charity's programmes. This is potentially a double exclusion, based both on not understanding others (because of a use of specialised language, or accent, or vocabulary) and on not being able to articulate what one wants to say. To try to get around this, Debbie and I invented a game for one training day, where the participants split into four groups. Each group had to invent five words and then use them in a sentence. The groups then shared their sentences and had to work out what the words meant. The aim was partly that the participants would be able to see that language is always changing, and to devise strategies for navigating words they did not know with more confidence.

The game was a reminder too that language is never inherently 'difficult', but that there is a question of whose language is in play at any time. I taught Nina for a module in the second year of her undergraduate course that introduced a range of ideas from literary theory. In one class, we were reading the postcolonial theorist Gayatri Chakravorty Spivak's (1988) essay 'Can the subaltern speak?'. Spivak is often noted for the difficulty of her writing; she has won the annual 'Bad Writing Award' from the *Journal of Philosophy and Literature*. The students in this seminar were all mature. There were two men and 13 women. Twelve of the students were White, two were African-Caribbean, and one was of Chinese origin. The White students dominated the discussion to begin with and their complaints against Spivak's style were insistent. "Why does she write this way?," one asked. "Shouldn't it be possible to say these things in a way that's comprehensible?," said another, to general approval. "This made me feel stupid," another student said quietly. Nina interrupted them. She had found plenty of the texts we had looked at in this module difficult. But now she said: "It didn't seem that difficult to me. She's saying 'fuck off', she's just saying it in her own way."

This is an extract from an interview with Nina, during the final year of her degree, in which she looked back on the same seminar in the context of her wider studies:

Q: "And was there anything about [studying] literature that you particularly enjoyed?"

N: "If I'm honest, I enjoyed all of it. It's been a struggle, but that's because – just the way my brain works and I have to accept that and that isn't necessarily the university's fault, and the baggage you carry from school or you've experienced in the past. It's taken me a long time to say: 'Ooh, hopefully now I can write!' I've always wanted to write, it's always been something in me. I've just always got bad feedback about it. I think everything you've done, even Shakespeare [laughs], has been *fine*. I struggled with some of it, I'm not going to lie. You might as well have been talking French. There were a couple of times I sat there and thought, "I don't even know what we're on about," but ... sometimes I'd get one thing. I remember one lecture you did, and I was like 'I get this,' and everybody was like 'I don't get it.' That was Spivak. I loved that."

Q: "So tell me why you got the Spivak when no-one else did."

N: "I just liked the way she writ. Some of it was hard but once I got into it, I loved what she was *saying*. And it was that stuff about other people – well, Europeans, coming in and then misplacing their ideas on to a community that has already been a community for hundreds of years and basically saying, 'What you do isn't correct,' but not looking at the cultural tradition. I'm like: 'Oh wow, that's happened here ....' Just that level of disrespect that's shown to people, it is that European perspective being put and you don't take the time to get to know that community, but you judge it, but because you have the power. So maybe *that* was what I understood. Somehow it connected for me.... I've got her books! And I wanted [to write] like her. I can't do it."

Q: "Yet."

N: "Yet – yeah! But I remember thinking, 'That's a model, or a way.' And she didn't use lots of big words, she used thoughts and ways, but I understood it. If you asked me what happened in the next lecture, I couldn't honestly say."[7]

We often frame a university education as being about students gaining 'academic literacy', learning how to speak, write and think as part of broader conversations and within given conventions. But Nina's experience with Spivak shows that there are many different kinds of literacy. Spivak's work has often been labelled as 'difficult', whereas to a student who had struggled with literacy issues and for whom some standard literary discussions 'might as well have been' in French, the same work offered 'a model, or a way'.

Philip Davis (2003) has written:

People are easily daunted and humiliated in educational institutions, when the assumption is that the ability to articulate is the first thing. It isn't: it is the second thing. The first thing is to have something to articulate, which inevitably at first must resist quick and easy formulation. (p 154)

It is also the case that what one wants to say may be compromised by the need to use language that lacks the terms or concepts one needs. Adrienne Rich's (1979) essay demonstrates the extent to which women navigating higher education must still do so within male language games. Nina's (sometimes painful) encounters with a literature syllabus show that a White language game can be similarly exclusionary.

★

For the Foundation Year in Arts and Humanities (FYAH) programme that we teach at Bristol, there is a skills course that covers topics such as library use, basic writing skills, taking notes in lectures, and reading difficult texts. One of the sessions is structured around two apparently simple questions: 'Why would someone speak in class?' and 'Why would someone be silent in class?' We always begin the session by asking the students if any of them has ever lost their voice. At least one person is usually able to describe the experience. In one year, a young woman called Cindy described opening her mouth and a whistling sound coming out where her voice should have been. She said that she had been working in a call centre at the time and "everyone I spoke to on the phone assumed I was a heavy breather". We then asked if anyone had ever found their voice. One year, Dennis, a man in his early twenties of mixed ethnic origin, talked about overcoming fierce and painful shyness as a teenager and suddenly discovering he had a voice.

The reasons students give for why one might speak in a seminar are always surprisingly varied. A woman called Lydia said that she might speak to inform others or exchange information. Others suggested they might speak to clarify something or offer an opinion, to interrupt, to question something, or to object to what has been said, either in the room or in what they had been reading. The students acknowledged the importance of emotions (excitement, enthusiasm or fear), as well as 'a desire to show off' as a motivation to speak. Cindy said that at school she had sometimes spoken because of peer pressure and fear of scrutiny. She said that she would feel relieved each time she spoke for the first time in a class, "because then I can relax". Dennis pointed out that one might speak for urgent practical reasons: if you needed to use the toilet, or to shout 'Fire!' Lydia asked aloud whether there might ever be a point you wished to make on the topic that could feel equally urgent.

The discussion of silence was especially moving. Students talked about being silent because they were processing complex information, or out of a desire to listen. Lydia and Cindy both came to a realisation about this, almost simultaneously. Lydia said she realised that silence can be a mode of participating. Cindy added that speech is not always a mode of engagement: it can be a way of dominating a situation. The students noted that silence can be generous (allowing others to participate); fearful (for example, a fear of giving offence); uncomfortable or physical (and that it might be due to a speech impediment, for example); or due to a lack of confidence. Some students also described enjoying silence, because it allowed them to think. A man called John, who had five children, said with a smile that silence was a rare experience in his life. Others spoke of being silent because they were distracted, tired, bored or hungover. A woman called Marie said she had not spoken for the first six weeks of the course, because she felt like an outsider, as if one half of her was still outside the room. Marie's comment led to another discussion. Another reason, I pointed out, why someone might be silent is if they were not in the room, whether temporarily or because they were not able to enter the university.

★

The first thing that we did when we were creating the foundation year was to write a series of about 60 pen portraits of fictional people who might be interested in joining the course. These were sometimes based on people we had met, taught, or heard about, while others were imagined. Richard Pettigrew drew partly on his own upbringing, having attended a comprehensive school in Scotland from which only a small number of students progressed to university. Tom Sperlinger drew especially on his background in adult education. The aim was to think of people who, for one reason or several, would not currently be in higher education. More broadly, it was our hope to think about those individuals and communities who, for whatever reason, are currently *least* likely to enter higher education, or a particular institution like Bristol – and then think about the kind of structural changes needed to include them. Two examples of the pen portraits are shown in Box 3.1.

Box 3.1: Fictional pen portraits

Sue

Age: 33

Brief biography: Sue is a recently divorced single mother with three young children. She left school at 16 with three GCSEs (Biology, History, Art). She works as a nursery nurse, but would ultimately like to retrain as a teacher. She enjoys art and has taken a painting course recently; she wonders if it might be possible for her to pursue an Art History degree, but is unsure if this would help her to become an art teacher or not.

How will she hear about the course? Sue's social networks are limited; she mainly interacts with co-workers at school or with other parents through her children's school.

Admissions issues: She would need to complete some written work as part of the process.

Fit with foundation year: A question mark here, as she might wish to pursue a more vocational course beyond the foundation year (for example, a degree with qualified teacher status). However, the possibility of going on to a degree for free is a huge attraction as finances are a major concern.

Commitment to foundation year, likely drop-out issues: Sue works part-time so would be able to attend two days per week, but is worried about managing the commitments required by the course with her work and children. She is also worried she will feel out of place if the other students are younger than her – she is concerned she may have left it too late to get a degree anyway.

Progression questions: Sue produces a good essay for the admissions work, but it shows some major problems with sentence construction, grammar and so on. The course would need to give her sufficient written skills to match her intelligence/thinking.

Andrew

Age: 23

Brief biography: Andrew left school before GCSEs because he never properly learned to read at school. He was functionally illiterate until two years ago; he attended further education college for literacy training and can now read well. Andrew doesn't have any specific plans for what he would like to do with his degree, but is interested in getting a university education. Andrew is currently a cook in the kitchens at the local secondary school.

How will he hear about the course? Through advertising to the school, hopefully. Andrew volunteers with the Black Development Agency and attended a taster course.

Admissions issues: Written work.

Fit with foundation year: Perfect.

Commitment to foundation year, likely drop-out issues: Andrew may find that university is just not what he imagined at all. He had a 'grass is greener' attitude to anything other than his current job, which he loathes. Having said that, he may remember how little he enjoyed his previous work.

Progression questions: Andrew's early problems with literacy will mean that he hasn't encountered written language for as long as the rest of his cohort. This could create problems for his written work.

We took these fictional portraits with us through each stage of the subsequent process. We thought about how each individual would hear about the course, which fed into the publicity we designed and the emphasis we placed on taster courses; we walked them through the admissions process, and tried to work out who would be admitted depending on how that process worked, which led to an emphasis on interview and written work (rather than on an application form alone); and then we designed the structure of the programme and the curriculum with these people in mind. Table 1 shows some of the key elements of the programme that emerged from this exercise. One argument we have made subsequently for the pen portraits is that they allowed us to counter potential stereotypes when we spoke to and interviewed potential applicants to the course because they gave us a 'counter-stereotypical' example: someone who was not a 'typical' applicant but to whose potential we were now more actively alert (McLellan et al, 2016, p 9). It is, of course, possible that the pen portraits also revealed some of our own latent prejudices.

Table 1: Issues influencing programme design for the Foundation Year in Arts and Humanities

Issue identified	Impact on design of programme
The people we wish to reach might not be looking for a course of this kind/ might not think they can apply	• An admissions process that emphasises that no prior qualifications are required. • A dedicated website with a related publicity campaign in local media. • Fostering of good relationships with local media, especially the local newspaper, the *Bristol Post*. • A series of taster courses (one-off days and eight-week courses) with local community organisations including the Single Parent Action Network (SPAN), the Meriton (an alternative education provider for teenage mothers) and Bristol Refugee Rights.
Potential student may have other commitments outside of studies	• The programme is taught Mondays and Tuesdays from 10am to 3pm. • Students are permitted to do up to 21 hours' paid work per week (instead of the standard 15).
Potential students may not know about arts/humanities disciplines	• The programme is structured around two 'period' modules called 'What Does it Mean to be Human?'. • Lectures on these modules introduce all disciplines in faculty; each lecture looks at how a different subject addresses this question. • A linked series of smaller-group seminars introduce related skills and small-group discussion of the issues. • The two modules are linked, with the first one starting in the present day (often with Hollywood film) and working back over 2,000 years by the end of the second. • The thematic question allows students to bring in prior life experience and knowledge as well.
Gaps in skills	• A compulsory introductory skills module including essay writing, library use, taking notes, 'finding your voice', careers and other topics.
Lack of preparedness for particular discipline/ subject at degree level	• Each student undertakes an individual project (a 3,000-word essay) in the discipline they plan to study at degree level, with one-to-one supervision from a PhD student as well as group seminars.

Issue identified	Impact on design of programme
Lack of confidence/ fear of not fitting in at university	• The programme is fully embedded into school/ faculty structures so students gain confidence from experience of being students at Bristol for a year prior to undergraduate study. • The cohort is relatively small (up to 30 students per year), which builds confidence and the sense of a network.
Financial risks	• The programme has a lower fee in acknowledgement that it is a transitional year towards the fuller commitment of a degree (£3,500 initially; it has now risen to £4,500 plus inflation). • An additional bursary was introduced, calculated to replace income from paid work for the hours students would spend on their studies (this was only maintained for the first two years of the programme).

The programme has been successful in recruiting the kinds of student we had hoped to find. The 2017 entry data (Box 3.2 and Figure 1) gives a typical snapshot. The outcomes for these students have also been pleasing (as Box 3.3 illustrates). Of the first cohort, six students graduated in July 2017, two with a first-class and four with an upper second-class degree. Two of these students have gone on to postgraduate study at Bristol. Yet the fact that only a minority of the students from the first cohort completed their degree within three years is also significant. A high number of this first cohort took a year out during their studies – sometimes to earn more money, or for health or family reasons – while a small number repeated a year or changed programme.

Box 3.2: Who are the students?

Of the 27 students who started the foundation year in 2017, 19 were over 21, of whom 10 were over 25 and four were over 40 (70/37/15%); 16 were from the Bristol area (59%); six were from Black or minority ethnic groups (22%); seven had a disability (26%); and 14 were from the first generation in their family to attend higher education (52%). Seventeen students were from NSeC categories 4-7 (63%), that is from families where the main profession is associated with lower socioeconomic groups. Twelve students were from Participation of Local Areas (POLAR) 1&2 (44%), postcodes where a low proportion of individuals go on to higher education, and eight were from POLAR 1 (30%), postcodes that are especially challenging for universities to recruit from. Fourteen students met four widening participation categories and three met six (52/11%). It is also noticeable that in all cohorts there has been a near 50-50 balance of men and women.

Figure 1: 2017 entrants to the Foundation Year in Arts and Humanities at the University of Bristol

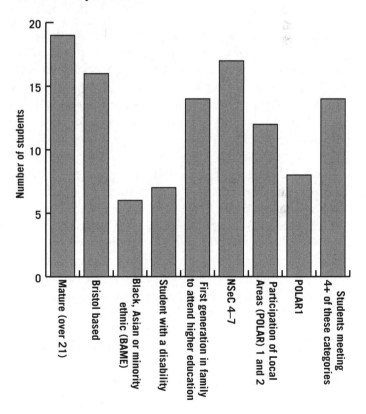

Box 3.3: What happens next?

One hundred and one students started on the foundation year in 2013-16. Eighty-three per cent had a successful outcome and 75% went on to a degree programme or similar qualification. This is comparable to similar programmes at Durham University, where 75-80% complete and 65-70% go on to degrees. Sixty-six students have gone on to 21 different degrees at Bristol and 10 to degrees/qualifications elsewhere. Of the 66 at Bristol, four have withdrawn or been deemed withdrawn (6%). Of the 17 students who did not complete the foundation year, two have subsequently gone on to study elsewhere.

To some extent, this programme illustrates Reay's arguments about the importance on focusing on inequalities and experiences within the system as well as access to it. Reay (2017) emphasises the higher levels of debt experienced by working-class students, especially since maintenance loans replaced grants, and the greater amount of paid work such students do (p 128). In a survey in 2017, we found that 58% of FYAH students undertook paid work during the programme itself, while three out of four did so on progressing to a degree. In 2015/16, a survey of first- and third-year undergraduates at Bristol was undertaken by the Personal Finance Research Centre in the School of Geographical Sciences. It found that one in four students overall were undertaking paid employment during term-time, compared with just under half of mature students and those not living in university halls (Butcher at al, 2017, p 18). Evidence suggests that inequalities can also continue after such students graduate from an elite university. Coulson and colleagues (2017) found that 57% of the working-class students on a special-entry scheme to an elite Russell Group university gained graduate jobs, compared with 74% of all graduates across the same university, even though more of the former group gained a first-class or upper second-class degree (pp 14-15).

In 2016, a number of students from the FYAH programme were interviewed as part of a wider project for the Office for Fair Access (OFFA) on outreach for disadvantaged adult learners (Butcher et al, 2017). Three clearly identifiable stages were evident in their experiences. Students spoke especially warmly about their experiences of short courses and tasters and about the fact that the programme admitted them without prior qualifications. Dave, who left school at 13 with a reading age of seven, noted: "I thought that somebody with no education, no qualifications ... wouldn't be any point applying to a degree. Which is why the foundation year was exciting because it was a route in." The location of the short courses was particularly significant as well as the staff who were involved in teaching them. For instance, Alice found the lecturer on the SPAN course particularly influential in terms of her decision to apply for the foundation year: "It's almost like it can be achieved now, here is this woman, she came into the inner city, she taught us, she's just so down to earth. It's not out of our range as it would normally be felt by us in the inner city." Students spoke in almost equally positive terms about the second stage: their experience of the foundation year itself. One student said, "I've actually earned my place now"; another commented that, "I've just found it to be an elixir ... it's just changed my whole wellbeing"; several noted the confidence it gave them in their own opinions: "I'm getting angles that academics don't, couldn't possibly get, because they haven't got that experience, life experience." This last example reveals the extent to which academics themselves can sometimes become a homogeneous group, in their life experiences and perspectives.

Yet the students sometimes related painful experiences in the transition from this programme to a degree. Some no longer felt they belonged with their new cohort, especially those who were older: "Me and the woman who also did the foundation year, sat in the middle row in the middle of the lecture theatre and then everybody else came in and there was this gap left around us. [laughing] Like a sort of exclusion zone." One woman spoke about how she felt life experience was less valued in discussions on her degree programme: "Then you feel you don't want to maybe give something of yourself, your life experience of whatever, because you don't know how it's going to be received ... almost like you've given part of yourself away really and it hasn't been reciprocated." Multiple difficulties were also reported around the structure of degrees, with students struggling to adapt to the workload, a more complex (and shifting) timetable, and also to the narrowness of a single disciplinary focus, after the interdisciplinary reach of the one-year programme.[8]

One could see this account of the FYAH students' experiences as the inevitable falling away of certain kinds of idealism, as one enters a large institution and institutional system. But for us it has also prompted another question. We (too often) think of the 'end' of this particular system – the degree – as its goal or culmination. But what if the students' experiences point to an inverted model, in which it is the taster courses outside the university where the most important educational experiments take place? Is there a way of recreating the spirit and structure of the tasters in a larger university system? The taster courses are free to those attending; are co-designed with a community organisation, and often with the participants themselves, and advertised jointly; are usually offered not in the university but in a community venue; and are non-accredited, so there is some freedom about what (if any) assessment is offered. All of this makes these courses inclusive in ways that a formal university programme tends not to be, and also creates a different spirit of intellectual enquiry.

This is how Mwenza Blell, an anthropologist, described her approach to one of the tasters she taught at a charity that supports refugees:

"I've always wanted to run a class where I asked students what they wanted to learn. I went in and gave an introductory lecture on anthropology, [and] talked a little bit about my research, which spans enough things that you get the feeling that there isn't anything off limits. Then I said, 'What do you want to talk about?' and every week we revisited that. 'What do you want to talk about next week? Do you still want to talk about this, this week?' I made some slides with some ideas and we just had a discussion for two hours around the things on the slides and it really took off. They really engaged with the idea that they were deciding what we talked about. Even though it was different people every week. There was a core of people."

The course began by discussing ideas around food, including its production and social uses, as well as economic questions. Blell notes that one question that was discussed was how food is shared, as the students noted that English people were less likely to share their food than in some other cultures. Later, the group considered whether there were alternative ways of running the world.

Blell's research continued to be important as a context for the discussions and she saw the tasters as an extension of it. This is an account of a similar course she ran with another charity:

"Sometimes, I'd present an idea that's an important idea in … my discipline. Just seeing what people [think] who are not primed to understand that idea as important. How does that match, or not match your experience? Or: where does an idea or what someone experiences as a fact come up against what you believe? That was really interesting and being able to make sure that didn't create unnecessary conflict in the space. Two twins who were from East Africa came who talked about how someone had done black magic on them when they were babies. I know enough about the political context that they come from to understand and place this idea but other people in the classroom were like, 'What? You say you were cursed?' [laughs]. Another woman was like, 'What if they told you that you'd die?' and I was like, 'Whoa, let me try to help us hold this conversation together.' I get what she's talking about, and it's interesting and I believe her, but I understand your response.

I saw one of the people from that class recently, I just ran into her. She really liked the class and it had been mind-expanding in that way, which made her want to study anthropology, that she was able to come away from something where she disagreed, with a much greater understanding that was more important than whether or not she disagreed with it. Seeing the way that happened and what kind of responses people had to things was really interesting to me from a research point of view, but seeing we could resolve that was also really important to me as an anthropologist. There's a bigger question – of the possibility of peace – that's in my mind. When we let everybody have a voice, can we get to a place where everybody has spoken and we can still all live with each other?"[9]

★

We began this chapter with Nina's story. In her reflections on her degree, Nina noted that one reason she had persisted with it was the community engagement element, in which she continued work with a Black women's arts organisation, with which she had been involved prior to beginning her studies. We discuss the structure of the community engagement modules on this degree in more detail in Chapter 7. There are compulsory modules in years 1-4 and students can devise and deliver their own project. Nina commented:

"It allowed me to be me. The other stuff I have to fit into a box, a box that sometimes you say 'Oh, it's about free thinking.' It is up to a point, but you have to conform. I think community engagement allowed me to explore and be with the community or to serve. I found that was the less structured part of the whole thing, so I could write, I could do a project, and you accepted me for me, what I did."

In a sense, the community engagement element of the programme allowed for some of the spirit of the tasters: co-created and less formal than what happens within a standard university space.

In the same cohort as Nina there was a student called Simon, who was in his forties. He had left school at the age of 12 and spent time in prison as a result of an alcohol and heroin addiction. He entered the university in his late thirties, first on a six-month, return-to-study course and then on the English Literature and Community Engagement degree. For his community engagement project, Simon set up a reading group with a Bristol-based charity that works with individuals affected by long-term poverty and issues such as addiction and mental health challenges. In the following interview excerpt, Simon describes perceptions of the university among people from that community:

S: "They were in a different place [from the university]. So two heroin addicts, no, three, one was like a real East London bank robber, just got out for bank robbery, was completely mad, and two long-term addicts. And I just showed up with some Charles Dickens. And [we] took it from there. I developed a structure to work within and handouts and exercises and encouraged people to ... go and find something."
Q: "And how did you know how to do all of that?"

S: "I think 50% of it was from my own experience with literature and my intuition with the people I was dealing with, just sussing out where they were coming from and using my experience of literature to see what would fit with them. And 50% of it was what I learnt at the university."

Q: "So, it was a real combination of life experience and what the university could offer?"

S: "Yeah, and because I was representing the university and I always had to remember that. I was a student from Bristol University but I was also trying to get across: 'I'm just like you.' And I knew that these guys were ... I knew what they were coming with [the attitude]: 'This is not for me, ah, it's alright for you.'" Somehow, they would have seen me as different because I'm representing Bristol University. So, I didn't want to go in there and tell my story like straight away, I wanted the literature to do the work, but over time, bit by bit, I would if I had to. And I have been known to get quite excitable and quite dynamic in a group. So, that transferred onto others in the group."

Q: "So, there's this perception that people at university are different to the likes of ...?"

S: "Yeah, I think there is. I think, you know, and it's completely wrong, you know, but I think a lot of disadvantaged communities are stuck in their own story."

Q: "What is that story?"

S: "It's a poverty story, it's a victim story, it's a self-pitier story, it's a limited story. There's no examples, you know, you can't say like 'Oh he went on and changed,' nobody changes their life."

Q: "And where does that come from? I know where poverty comes from but where does the victim [come from]?"

S: "Well if you find yourself in prison over and over and over again, if you find yourself on the streets or if you're a girl who's been abused, domestic violence over and over again, it's just part of it. You start to believe you're no good and, you know, which isn't true but it can be very wearing for them and for everybody else…. It's like you'd ask them, 'What do you think of Bristol University?,' and they'd say: 'It's nothing to do with me.'"

Q: "Why is it nothing to do with them?"

S: "Because it's not their world. That's for other people. That's for people with money or not bringing in certain education, you know."

Q: "So, it's in the city but it's not …?"

S: "It's up on a hill. It's not in the … yeah, it's not part of the city. It was always, you know, it's on the hill. Whereas now, you know, it's very easy for me to walk down [the road in the university] now. It doesn't feel foreign. But I can remember at first, it's an intimidating, you know, place and that's why people …"

Q: "Why is it intimidating?"

S: "Because, again, it's not yours, it's not for you, you know, somehow you stand out, you know. That's what I felt. It doesn't matter [now]. I can walk in there now to…. You know, I'd feel guilty at first, walking in through by the two security guys. I'm like, 'What would they do if I'm in here robbing?', or 'What's he want?' But that's the experience of a lot of these guys if you ask them. They say: 'Oh I don't belong here. Somebody's going to tap me: "Can I help you?"' Well I can walk in here now [head] held

> high: 'Alright guys, good afternoon.' I don't need
> to explain myself. It's my university. (Cited from
> unpublished research for Butcher et al, 2017)

The discussion with Simon frames many of the issues that we discuss in this book. Why is it that some people feel that a university is 'not mine', is 'nothing to do with me', is 'not my world'? Is it possible for someone in that situation to enter the university without feeling they must relinquish what they have experienced, known and valued beforehand, but instead to have something like the fifty-fifty relationship between education and experience that Simon describes here? How can any knowledge that is acquired in a formal learning environment interact with intuitions and experiences learned outside it? And how can these two worlds that are so foreign to one another – the university and the city; the university and the community – come to speak to one another, so that others can, like Simon, (literally) walk between them and feel a sense of belonging in each, creating their own story in the process?

The stories Simon tells above illustrate this in their own way, showing communities able to interact with universities on their own terms, whereas Reay and others have shown how often an individual working-class or Black student may feel isolated in navigating an institution on their own, and may be more likely to drop out. Nina's account of her experiences shows the limits there are currently to how far a Black, female, part-time mature student can feel part of a university like Bristol.

Yet Simon's story also illustrates the importance of rethinking how we measure achievement. Simon had to withdraw from his degree in the fourth year due to a serious health condition. He is thus an example of why part-time study is now seen as a risk to universities, which are scrutinised on the percentage of students completing their degrees. His work with this charity led on to multiple collaborations with the university, including the time I spent there as a researcher. As a consequence of his work and that of the charity, more than 30 students now at university or a further education college owe their journey back into education, formally or informally, in part to the reading group they set up. But Simon is recorded on a spreadsheet, for his engagement with his degree, as an 'unsuccessful leaver'.

4

Education and the shape of a life

"It wasn't right for me back then."

This is Jack, Trevor, Zara, Sasha, or any number of adult learners. Many come back into education because they always wanted to go to college or university, but couldn't when it might have been available to them earlier. They were starting a family, perhaps; or they suffered illness or bereavement; they had to care for a family member or they needed to earn money; or perhaps they had an undiagnosed learning difficulty such as dyslexia. But many also come back into education because only now have they decided they want to study something in particular, or see study in general as relevant to their lives. Some had other particular interests they wished to pursue – a career in football or cricket or acting, perhaps (all of which might be educational in their own ways). Others just felt that the world of work would suit them better.

Were they wrong? Are they only now realising that they would have been better off back then trying to go to college or university? We think not. People are wonderfully diverse, and the shape of an individual life is determined by an enormous range of factors. Some people who wish to become parents want to do it quite quickly, in their late teens or early twenties; others prefer to wait a few years; some wish to wait much longer. Some people want, or get stuck with, the same job for their whole working life; others pursue a number of different careers. None of these trajectories is better than any other – there is no ideal life-shape towards which we all should strive – and each of them may be more or less of a conscious choice. And this is no less true of the timing of university study. Some people are ready at 18 years old, or perhaps 19 or 20 after spending time outside education for one or two years. And they're ready for the full-time three- or four- or even five-year undergraduate programme. For others, that's not the right time. They are coming out of 14 years of highly directed education. Why not wait a little before embarking on three or four years more? And why not undertake that education in stages – a year of study in the evening here, in your late thirties; six months full-time study there, in your forties, on a career break; and two years full-time later, in your fifties, after your children have left home?

In Chapter 3, we explored why shorter forms of provision may create different possibilities – intellectually, pedagogically, and for an individual student – from a long-form degree structure. We also saw an example, in Simon, of someone whose achievements spread out well beyond the standard classification of a degree, but were not recognised formally by that award. Is it possible, therefore, to imagine a different kind of system, in which the shape of educational institutions is much more responsive to the various kinds of lives we lead?

This is not a new task. The Dearing Report (1997) articulated the need for a 'learning society' in the UK and for higher education institutions to recognise the value of lifelong learning. Dearing thought this meant that universities needed to 'structure qualifications which can be either free-standing or built-up over time, and which are commonly accepted and widely recognised' and to 'offer opportunities for credit transfer between courses and institutions' (1997, para 1.18). Yet the

20 years since then have seen, at best, partial success in these areas. An institution such as the Open University makes broad use of credit transfer and accumulation mechanisms (whereby students can move between universities and take their credits with them), but the Russell Group (2016) remains largely hostile to these ideas. Meanwhile, the tuition fee system that Dearing also proposed has, over time, fed a drive towards much greater homogeneity in qualifications, with more and more of what is offered becoming 'degree shaped'. There is substantial evidence that this disadvantages adult learners, as Claire Callender (2017) and others have shown.

We speak often these days of different types of learner. They tend to be categorised according to the sense through which they learn best, so that visual learners retain information better when it is presented in a diagram or a chart or an animation, while auditory learners learn best from material they hear. But, of course, there are many other dimensions along which our approach to learning might differ. Some people learn best when they are given problems to solve – here are some facts about a country, now design a voting system for it that is as fair as possible; here's a brief for a smartphone app to combat social isolation, now build it on this platform. Others learn best from purely theoretical presentations – here are some formal results in voting theory and some debates about the value of democracy; here are sociological perspectives on the causes and effects of loneliness; here are the developer tools for this mobile operating system. Some learn better when they are engaged in debate and discussion with others; others when they are reading in a library on their own. And, of course, each student might find that what suits them best changes over time, as they become more comfortable in a particular study environment, or are in other ways happier or sadder (or hungrier, or more tired) and depending on the particular material with which they are working.

All of these differences are local and concern the micro-environment of learning; they are differences in what is going on for the person at the time they're doing it. But what about the macro-environment? There are some for whom three years of full-time study unaccompanied by other work is a dream, a gift, the perfect environment, while others loathe it, finding it overwhelming or agoraphobic, and involving too much time devoted to one thing. Indeed, it's interesting that even research-focused academics themselves – the people you might expect to be selected precisely because of their fit with the traditional mode of engagement with higher education – often report finding research sabbaticals unproductive and intimidating precisely because they entail too much time focused on a single pursuit. And this is in spite of such sabbaticals being at a premium, and a very desirable mode of working, at least in theory. So, just as some people learn better looking at a chart and others listening to a lecturer and others debating and others making, so some get more from their time at university when it is pursued to the exclusion of all else, and others when it is pursued alongside a career or raising a family or volunteering. And not when these other parts of life are crammed in around the meagre margins of a full-time degree, but rather when each occupies its own space comfortably.

But this is about more than making part-time degrees available more widely. We aren't just proposing that we create more opportunities to study four, six or more years back-to-back, studying half-time or less, with work and life given greater room to breathe. For many, that is too long, too daunting – it stretches off into a future they've hardly begun to anticipate or imagine. What's more, its formal rewards (as we saw in Chapter 3) hang simplistically on lasting the course – a miss, for such degrees, like for three-year full-time degrees, is as good as a mile. Instead, we are proposing a model in which we think primarily in terms of what universities currently call 'units' or modules – single topics, such as an introductory module on Mengzi's ethics, or Shakespeare's tragedies, or algebraic geometry, or special relativity theory – rather than what they call 'programmes' – whole degrees, such as a BA in History or a BSc in Experimental Psychology. Modules become the standard unit of study, not degree programmes. People accumulate these modules during the course of their lives – as many or as few as they wish to.

This would also leave much more space for these individual modules to be more flexible in mode and structure, and in how they are created. There would be a lot more space for experimentation, with individual modules being co-designed (perhaps quite quickly) with charities, community organisations, social enterprises, industries, multinational corporations, or regional and local governments, in response to emerging needs and questions. There would also be much more space for modules that are deliberately open-ended in the questions they ask, as in Mwenza Blell's example in Chapter 3, and which thus design and decide the questions they ask in collaboration with the students who attend, making their life experience a key part of what shapes the module. Such a mode is particularly appropriate in adult education, in which the experience of the learners may be so varied and is likely to be less predictable than in a class of 18-year-olds who have followed broadly comparable educational journeys. This is also where students themselves could be involved as 'producers', with a significant portion of their studies given over for practice, practical work or engagement, with Simon's reading group in Chapter 3 as only one of the possible examples.

Box 4.1: How would a modular system work in practice?

The modular system we are proposing is linked to how we think the system might be funded. We propose that every individual physically present in the UK, regardless of their circumstances – whether permanent resident, citizen, refugee, asylum seeker, displaced person or migrant – should be entitled to up to 60 credits for free, pursued either in a further education college or a higher education institution.

Beyond that 60 credits, there would then be a limited number of 'specialism' routes, into which students would be admitted more formally. This would include standard professional routes, including carpentry, design, law, medicine, veterinary sciences, dentistry, nursing and social work. These routes would have very specific links between modules and particular requirements for professional accreditation. But there would be considerable advantages to not having a formal endpoint – the award of a degree – as currently, since students could continue much more easily to accumulate additional credit across their career (indeed, this would become the norm).

There would then be an extremely wide range of generalist modules, offered both within and across currently disciplinary boundaries, and with each student choosing their own route through the subsequent options.

Of course, certain subjects are more 'cumulative' than others. For instance, the topics currently covered in a second-year module on statistics may well presuppose knowledge gained in the first-year statistics module. To accommodate this, in our proposed system, some modules would have prerequisites – that is, you wouldn't be able to study it without having previously studied some other module. So first-year statistics might be a prerequisite for second-year statistics; the module on special relativity might be a prerequisite for the module on general relativity.

We discuss the question of admission beyond 60 credits in Chapter 5.

The benefits of such a system accrue not only to those whose learning style is better suited to a macro-environment that includes other pursuits beyond the academic. It also suits those whose lives cannot fit study any other way – those with families, obligations to care for loved ones who are ill, elderly, or disabled, those with financial needs that can't be covered by student loans, or who would rather not get involved in that system. It suits those who change their minds about what they want to do, or who simply get it wrong first time around. Cleo, for instance, who joined the army straight out of school, but became disillusioned with that life and realised that she craved learning again, or who discovered an interest in history as she travelled across the world with her battalion. Jake, another example, who pursued a semi-professional rugby career for a short time, focusing all his energies on that, but soon wanted something else. Did Jake and Cleo change their minds, or did they come to know their own minds better? It's always hard to tell. But, whichever it is, the current system excludes them, or at best deters them.

Jake and Cleo are also both individuals who are in a position to make choices. One of the other questions here is the extent to which choices may be determined for an individual by circumstances beyond their control. Lizzie Brown, whose story we considered in the Introduction, wished to go to university, and had the family support and academic record to do so. But, as a woman from a poor family, the system gave her limited options. There are others for whom the system – or circumstances – militate against choosing to go to university much earlier on.

Perhaps the most important change we suggest making to the university system is to make it much more responsive to the endlessly complicated ways in which people's lives unfold, and how they learn from that. This means making the choice to go to university as widely available as possible, and in modes that are quickly responsive to the urgent questions that arise in the middle of a life. So if Cleo in fact left the army in part through grief at the death of a friend – or at her own role in the death of an 'enemy combatant' – she might find a course on military history, or the philosophy of death that would be responsive to the new concerns she had discovered. Similarly, if Jake left rugby and worked for a charity supporting children to live heathier lives, he might find he needed access to research that would help him support the charity's aims or its business ambitions. It also means that someone for whom education seems irrelevant at 16 does not close off all their options by leaving school at that point, and that someone who only escapes a controlling father in their late twenties is not left with the choices that were made for them by an abusive parent. We explore these questions in more depth in the fictional case studies in Box 4.2.

Box 4.2: Examples of modular learning stories

Rafeef arrives in the UK as an asylum seeker, fleeing a civil war in her home country. She spends five years in the UK, before returning to her home country after the war has ended. She speaks little English, and initially her engagement with education is based on acquiring language skills. She has the equivalent of GCSEs in her home country. In her final year in the UK, by which times she is fluent in English, Rafeef takes three 20-credit modules for free in international law. When she returns to her home country, she continues her studies and puts these 60 credits towards a qualification in law. She completes further units, at the equivalent of postgraduate study, through a university in the UK and with the support of her employer, studying online.

Tim leaves school with three A-Levels, in English, History and French. He wants to go to university, but is unsure what to study. He takes three 20-credit modules in astrophysics, economics and theatrical performance, because he wants to broaden his options. He takes these modules at the university closest to his home town, while working part-time and volunteering in the community. He decides to move away from home for university, but opts to live in shared student/social housing, and to pay his rent by volunteering in two capacities in this accommodation, which houses elderly people and in which vulnerable young people engage in a range of activities, including theatre. Tim pursues modules across a wide range of subjects, but makes economic history a particular focus. He starts to build in teaching-training modules in his third year, and then continues with modules in Black British history, after he has started his first teaching role at a school with a high Black British population.

Jenny leaves school at 16. She grows up in care and wants to move to a different town, to start a new life. She works in a variety of part-time, seasonal and short-contract roles, while she tries to work out what she wants to do in the long term. In her early twenties, Jenny is in a relationship with a woman who has children, and there is pressure for them both to be earning more money. Jenny gets a job as a receptionist at a nursery and becomes interested in the work that is going on with the children. Her employer encourages her to enrol for courses at the local university. She takes an introductory 20-credit module in childcare, on which she hears about some ideas from psychoanalysis that are new to her, and is drawn particularly to the work of psychoanalyst Karen Horney. Having sought advice from the university, Jenny takes another module on introductory psychoanalysis, and then a third module on film, which she did not realise you could study. These studies take Jenny about two years, at the end of which her relationship breaks down. Jenny spends about five years in what she later calls a 'wilderness', experimenting with recreational drugs, losing her job and having periods during which she is homeless. At around this time, Jenny starts to read about psychoanalysis again, after visiting a local library. She moves town and enrols in her local university on an intensive but generalist study route, in which she pursues modules in film and psychoanalysis full-time over two years. During this time, she becomes active in student politics, and she continues with some individual modules in psychology. She hopes to run for election as a local councillor.

The current system: a thought experiment

So these are some of the individuals who are served poorly by the timeframes on which a university education is undertaken under the current regime. But who does it serve well? It is instructive to indulge a small thought experiment here. Just as we are exploring in this book what sort of university system would suit the sort of beings we are and the sorts of societies we have formed, so we might turn the question on its head and ask what sort of beings suit the current higher education system.

As previously noted, the sort of person for whom the current university system is well designed will be a certain sort of learner. They will also be someone who knows at exactly the right time what they would like to study and how. Aged 13, they will know whether they want to go to university and, if they do, what they want to study when they're there. After all, as Wendy Piatt makes clear in the quotations in the Introduction (and as Mary Beard reiterates in an exchange with David Lammy, cited below), they must choose their GCSEs appropriately. Aged 15, they will pick their A-Levels to suit the degree they'd like to do. Aged 17, they'll study for and sit those A-Level exams in good health and with a stable home life, so that their marks will correctly measure their abilities. Aged 18 or 19, they will start their degree and they will move with only minor obstacles to its conclusion three or four years later, where they will graduate successfully. In short, their young life – mid-teens to early twenties – will have a very particular shape. Such a shape is also suggestive of a certain kind of conformity to a system – in order to achieve in it, or out of lack of thought to alternatives – that, extrapolated to its natural endpoint, is potentially frightening: a dystopia of beings who may not have learned to think for themselves (see Arendt, 1971). And it suggests a further risk, since it reminds us that in the current system it is possible to only or mostly encounter others in the classroom who are following a similar route to your own.

It is a shape, it should be said, to which universities typically cater not because of some immutable feature of the human lifecycle. Rather, it is a shape that was determined by historical accident and preserved by tradition. In the 1590s, people matriculated to Oxford at any age between 15 and 18, but by the 1600s, there was a concentration of 17-year-olds. When universities provided only vocational training, for the church or the law or for medicine, the shape made a little more sense, although it has long been argued that life experience is also invaluable in these professions. People needed the training before they could pursue their career in these areas. But as the liberal idea of higher education emerged – from Newman and others – and universities evolved and became places in which people could explore the rich and vast array of human knowledge, and as many employers came to prefer providing in-house training for their new recruits, the shape lost its original motivation.

As the nature of professional life alters again, with the onset of what many are calling a fourth industrial revolution, it is likely to change once more, with many more people needing to change career or reskill in the middle of their life, even where they are pursuing what used to be a lifelong profession. But inertia has preserved the existing model, and attempts to change it (including Dearing's) foundered because it was a route that many middle-class young adults could pursue, whether or not pursuing it was in their best interests. So what we have now is a university system designed to fit a conception of a life that grew out of the norms and societal structures of a different time.

Something similar can be said about the traditional model of much white-collar work: full-time, 9-to-5 working almost exclusively in the office, weekends off, a few weeks of paid holiday per year. There is nothing timeless or inevitable about this model, which is the product of a particular combination of social, economic and technological change, government legislation and trade union activism. In recent years, both employers and employees – each for their own reasons – have begun to demand more flexibility, leading to a rise in part-time, job shares, flexible hours, working from home, and the option to purchase more holidays than the basic allowance, or to take longer periods as career breaks. Part of our argument is that universities need to make similar changes to the modes of study that they offer and, through that, to other aspects of what they do: how they support staff (who might also wish to be students), how they interact with other organisations in their city or region, and how they create knowledge in the classroom and in research.

So the sort of being for whom the current university system is perfectly designed is a certain sort of learner and their young life has a certain sort of shape. But even among those who meet this demanding specification, there will still be many who are poorly served by the system. In their early twenties, these people emerge from 17 years or so of primary, secondary and tertiary education. To be the sort of being for whom the current system is the ideal design, such a person must never be in need of higher education again. They must be the sort of person who has extracted all they would ever need from a university education within the three or four years they spend pursuing it at the tail end of their teens; and they must be able to store what they have gleaned, in perfectly useable form, for the rest of their lives. That is too tall an order for nearly all of us. The sorts of skills and knowledge, the insights and perspectives we take away from a university education, like those we take from our time at primary and secondary school, must be practised and honed or we lose them.

Education and 'a good life'

Much of life – much of modern tech-filled life, particularly – is too full to seriously use the skills learned at university very often. And then, when something happens that calls for just those skills, they are rusty; or when something calls for that knowledge, it is gone or only dimly remembered; or perhaps you didn't learn it in the first place, because you studied something else first time around. Perhaps a major political event occurs and you want to evaluate it – the rise of the far right, the failure of climate treaty negotiations, the apparent breakdown of investigative journalism – but your original study does not equip you for this. You want to learn about historical precedents, perhaps, but you studied mathematical physics; you want to know about the technology that underpins some of the developments, how it works and what it can do, but you studied philosophy; you want to learn new concepts – the Overton window, the banality of evil, intersectionality, toxic masculinity – with which you might think through the issues, but you studied pharmacology; you want to learn the science of climate change – you want to learn how greenhouse gases warm the earth, how models that are known to be inaccurate in various ways can nonetheless give reliable predictions, what tipping points are and which are more likely than others – but you studied Classics.

You wouldn't tolerate a healthcare system that excluded you from medical treatment until you're 60 years old on the grounds that that is when most people will most need it. Why, then, do we tolerate an education system with an analogous structure? Partly, I think, because of how we view education and its role in living a good life. Recent times have seen much greater recognition in Western countries that mental well-being is as crucial for a good life as physical well-being; an acknowledgment that the enormous advances in treatment for somatic suffering count for little if the longer, more dependable, more pain-free lives they afford us are not happy or fulfilled. Self-help books and well-being policies abound; yoga, mindfulness and meditation have entered the mainstream from their previous place in alternative and new age culture; the UK Labour Party and the Scottish government have appointed ministers and shadow ministers for mental health. There has been considerable research suggesting that education, and adult education in particular, has wider health benefits (see Lear, 2016). But this has not often made it into mainstream discussion. A notable exception was Vince Cable's (2010) description of his mother, at a time when he was secretary of state with responsibility for higher and further education:

> My mother and father left school at 15 to work in factories. My father eventually taught building trades in the local technical college: we need more people like him. My mother was a housewife and when I was 10 she had a major nervous breakdown and spent time in a mental hospital. When she recovered she saved her mind through adult education – learning for the first time about history, literature, philosophy and art. We need more people like her, too.

Perhaps the problem in recognising experiences like this comes because its effects seem too indirect, and the gratification too delayed – mindfulness apps promise results in weeks, and education can't compete with that turnaround. Perhaps it's because it isn't so easily monetised – it is easier to sell individual books and apps than whole courses of study. Perhaps. Though education does enrich a life quickly; and many companies have been very successful in turning a profit from it. Cable's point was also that, 'Education for education's sake – learning how to learn – benefits the economy in the long term.'

A major part of the problem is that we simply don't talk of education as having the function of helping us to live. In much public discussion, education is portrayed as something that equips you with a certain sort of technical skill that you'll need in adult life – literacy, for instance, or numeracy, or a certain sort of knowledge that might inform later decisions you make as a citizen – historical or scientific information, perhaps. When people bemoan falling standards in our primary and secondary educational systems, they talk of poor grammar or mental arithmetic, a lack of knowledge of the Tudors, or Soviet communism, or the Industrial Revolution, perhaps an ignorance of basic evolutionary science. But education can offer much more than this. As the Marmot Review (2010) showed, two thirds of our health and well-being is driven by social factors, with only a third driven by 'clinical' factors – and 'empowerment' is vital to health.

Let's consider an example. A great deal of stress in life arises from the feeling that we are not in control of the forces that affect our lives. In the past, these forces came from the natural world – unpredictable weather that devastated crops, infections and viruses, epidemics that wiped out families, explosions and collapses in coal mines – as well as from the political and the social spheres – government decisions, breakdowns in personal relationships, the effects of discrimination and oppression. As we have come to understand the natural world better and to believe we can tame it, the natural forces cause less stress than before – the medical state of the poorest in Britain in 2017 is better than the richest in 1817, and the richest in 1817 were very rich indeed. But the political and social forces still impinge significantly. And much of the stress they cause arises from a feeling that they are not only out of our control, but also beyond our ken. Indeed, as democracy has expanded, one can argue that more people are in control of the political forces that govern them than ever before; and yet the political, economic and social worlds have become so much more complex that the decisions on which we vote democratically lie further beyond our understanding than they have ever done. Many of us feel bewildered trying to understand how inflation works and what policies might drive changes in it. We feel completely at sea thinking about what short selling is and how it might be regulated, or whether a country should join a currency union or a trading bloc or not, or whether quantitative easing is a reasonable strategy following a recession, and so on. It is no longer possible to be a 'Renaissance wo/man' and know a little about everything and the latest developments in most fields. At the same time, there is an urgent need to prepare ourselves for how the natural world is already starting to overwhelm our capacity to understand it again, as a consequence of climate change. And climate change is a key educational challenge, because an understanding of it depends on both highly specialised knowledge and on being able to relate to the world in a way that moves beyond how it is immediately seen and experienced.

It is not just climate change, or economic policy with its daunting mathematical component, that are opaque to many of us. Think of social problems, such as homelessness, social isolation and increasing trends in male suicide. As activists in these areas will attest, the forces that drive these societal tragedies are very complex and the solutions not always obvious. Or think of the rise of the political far right in Europe and the US. It is terrifying to many, and part of the terror stems from the fact that we don't understand it. Is it a backlash against multiculturalism? Is it driven by economic pressures on White working-class people? Or are the newly emboldened White supremacists driven by a sense that their identity is under threat? Or their privilege? Or have these attitudes existed all along, only recently rehabilitated as acceptable in mainstream political discourse? Or think more local; closer to home. Think of your angst in the face of your own mortality, or your questing after a life that is meaningful in the face of a godless universe; your sense of your place in the human world.

All of these puzzles – the political, the economic, the social and the personal – cause anxiety and stress. And yet all are studied in universities – whether in economics or politics departments, philosophy or English literature departments, history, art history, or modern languages departments. A university is, after all, simply an institutionalised version of our puzzling. Higher education can give us the knowledge and the tools to address many of these issues, particularly if it is reshaped so that the charities, social workers, businesses and ordinary people who experience their effects could be involved in the study of their causes, and thus in asking different questions about the range of solutions that is available.

Vocational study

Before we leave this discussion of the shape of university study and the way in which it should interweave with the other threads of our lives, let's consider vocational degree programmes – medicine, law, dentistry, veterinary science; perhaps also engineering and psychology. How might they fit within the new flexible schedules we are proposing? Could a student really become a qualified doctor by accumulating modules over a 20-year period that amount to the same content as is covered on a standard five-year medical degree? It may well turn out that they could not. The sort of knowledge amassed in these modules is likely of the use-it-or-lose-it variety – take a break from studying for three years while you build your family, perhaps, or care for an infirm parent, and it fades so dramatically that you cannot be relied on to know it when the time comes. Perhaps this is particularly true of the practical, manual skills learned on hospital rotations. The model we propose would respect this. Our goal is not to impose a certain degree of flexibility at all costs, regardless of whether it is in tension with the purpose of the course of study. But while the flexibility that we would hope to see in arts and humanities, social science, and science courses might not be available in all vocational degrees, some of it must be; and it is possible that bespoke models of flexibility will emerge in these cases. Peter Raven (2014) already argues that medical schools should follow in their undergraduate programmes the less-than-full-time models that have been developed in postgraduate medical study. More recently, Ian Cumming, head of Health Education England, endorsed this, proposing further that it should be possible for those working in the health service already but not as doctors – nurses, for instance, or physician associates – to study part-time alongside their current role to become one (Matthews-King, 2017).

There are other reasons, in fact, why changes of this kind are likely to be pursued regardless of the benefits to inclusion (or with those as an incidental effect). The National Health Service (NHS) will see significant drops in available nursing and doctor staff following the UK's withdrawal from the European Union, and Cumming's proposals are intended to provide a new source of staff to make up the shortfall. This points to another argument in favour of change – an economic argument. Just as many were won over to women's participation in the labour market for capitalist reasons – the expanded workforce was a boon to companies, not least because they paid the newly employed women less than their male colleagues for doing the same work – it may be that similar ideas to those we propose will, in fact, be implemented because they would allow for a more flexible workforce, one that can retrain to exploit economic possibilities with greater agility. This may, ironically, create a need for something akin to the NHS University, which was proposed in the late 1990s, but which met with almost wholesale resistance at the time (see Taylor et al, 2010).

Cumming's vision of nurses training part-time alongside their job to become doctors also mirrors the 'degree apprenticeship' scheme launched by the UK government in 2015. These allow people to work full-time while undertaking part-time study towards a degree. The fees are paid by the employer and the degree must advance the employee's knowledge or skills in some way that will equip them better to do their job. As a result, they are currently available only for employees of major corporations – for example, Serco, BAE, Siemens – and only in a relatively select number of technical degrees courses, such as civil engineering, cybersecurity, digital and technology solutions.

These schemes identify and address the same problems as this book: the current overemphasis on full-time academic study, and the lack of part-time alternatives that can be easily combined with paid work. If the progress they make towards addressing these problems is relatively small, that is a further sign of the peculiar distinctions the UK system continues to make between vocational and academic qualifications. Why is it that we see the latter as more prestigious for young people to pursue, and the former as the only appropriate route for adult learners or those who have left school early? In part, as Reay and others have noted, this represents a class-oriented understanding of which individuals (and communities) should pursue particular kinds of study.

Our hope is that not only technical degree programmes with job-specific, practically implementable knowledge would be available to those wishing to study part-time, but also pure mathematics, sociology, history, chemistry or economics. There should also, we think, be much greater cross-pollination between different routes, so that those pursuing a particular vocational training leave themselves open to the possibility that they – like most of us – will need to retrain in future.

Small is beautiful

In the course of our careers, we have encountered people who have enrolled on short programmes of study for a variety of reasons. There was the young woman who had been brought up by her father, a single parent, and who had a breakdown when he nearly died. She studied literature and it gradually encouraged her to return to the vocation she had chosen, as a nurse. There was the young lawyer, who had chosen her career under family pressure and who, after taking a short history course, changed career and retrained as a journalist. There was the young man who had suffered from agoraphobia, for whom an evening class was the first time he made friends as an adult. Or the woman in her seventies, who made pottery in an evening class, after her studies on an art course in her teens were disrupted by war and migration. As these examples make clear, not all of this study happens within universities, and one benefit to the changes we propose is that universities would be much more closely aligned with further education colleges (with whom they might ultimately merge) and smaller providers. There would also be an opportunity to rethink the distinctions between formal and informal, academic and vocational, and 'useless' and 'useful' learning.

Alan Tuckett, who has written extensively on 'seriously useless learning', gives a further example, drawing on the traditional cliché of adult education as focusing on economically useless topics such as flower arranging:

> In 1991, the government wanted to stop funding adult education of all sorts. So we found a Brixton [in south London] florist who'd been a merchant banker and went to evening classes to learn floristry. He ended up

employing half the class, all of them men, most previously unemployed, in a shop opposite Brixton tube, in the heart of where the riots were in those days. That's the beauty of adult education. It's where people of different social classes meet and learn about one another. What happens on a wet Wednesday night in January doesn't make headlines but it can change lives. (Cited in Wilby, 2014)

One of the peculiarities of the university system is that it has the potential to be economically transformative on a broad scale. Arguably, this potential has not been realised precisely because universities have failed to learn lessons from other sectors in which 'different social classes meet and learn about one another'; in which the employed meet the unemployed; and in which incidental aspects of our lives come into the foreground of them.

Tuckett is also an especially persuasive advocate of the *narrative* aspects of adult education, the stories that emerge from it. If these stories are important – and many of those Tuckett tells are moving, inspiring or thought-provoking – it is partly because they foreground the extent to which our lives are shaped by complex forces, weave in and out of our control, and get entangled with other lives around them. It is time our education system likewise came to reflect the messy, complex, and often beautiful, shape of a life.

5

False negatives: on admissions

University lecturers in the humanities don't often find themselves awarding a mark of 85 out of 100 to the first essay a student produces at university – in fact, in those subjects, marks like that are pretty rare at any point. That early in their university career, most students are caught up in the enormous transition from one lifestyle – living with parents and going to school every day – to another – living in halls of residence, surrounded by new people, and often with much less structure to their daily routine. But, as I re-read this essay, marking it up with comments as I go, I can see that it's out of the ordinary, really exceptionally good. When I finish, I fish out the form the student completed when she applied to the Foundation Year in Arts and Humanities at the University of Bristol. The front page, where we asked applicants to detail any prior qualifications, was pretty sparsely populated: no A-Levels; a brief roster of GCSEs. Further in, however, there was the personal statement, a heartfelt plea to be taken seriously as a candidate, and it rang with the same originality and insight as the essay I had just marked. The student had been gripped by the guiding question for our course, 'What does it mean to be human?' She had become vegan the previous year, she explained, and had been trying to puzzle out our place among non-human animals, and the respect we owe to them. She had convinced herself that, as a species, we are far too impressed by the differences between ourselves and other animals, and far too ignorant of what we share in common; and she wanted to know whether this was a Western trait only or whether other cultures share it.

What does this show? On its own, not very much. Yes, nearly all universities base their admissions criteria on the results of prior qualifications their applicants have obtained at school or college – most often A-Levels or the International Baccalaureate, but also GCSEs, BTECs, Access courses, Cambridge's STEP exam, and so on. Clearly this student would most likely not have been offered a place at any university, and almost certainly would not have gained admission to Bristol, if it hadn't been for this non-traditional way in. But the problems with university admissions go beyond their reliance on prior educational achievement. Even the staunchest defender of our current university admission system will admit that even on its own terms it does not work perfectly: it offers places to some students who struggle with the intellectual content of the degrees they pursue; and it excludes some who would thrive in a university environment. In statistics, we call these Type 1 and Type 2 errors, respectively. The first are *false positives* – where a test admits a person who shouldn't have been admitted. The second are *false negatives* – where a test rejects a person who should have been admitted. This chapter is about the false negatives in our university admissions system, and how we might reduce the rate at which they are excluded.

There are many ways someone can become a 'false negative' in the existing university system. A few years ago, a reference arrived on the day of the deadline for applications for the part-time English Literature and Community Engagement degree at Bristol. The reference was for a mature student, Carol, from her then tutor on an Access course. It stated that Carol had gained very positive marks, shown intellectual curiosity, had an excellent attendance record, and got on very well with her fellow students. It seemed as if this was a dream applicant. There was just one problem: we couldn't find Carol's application form. Having searched our desks, the post room, several administrative offices, bags (several times over), and even kitchens and bookshelves at home, I swallowed my pride and rang her referee, to apologise that the application had been lost and to ask if he, or Carol, had a copy. The referee rang back almost straight away. When we had spoken the first time, he had been sure that Carol would have a copy, so it seemed likely that he would now say that he had it to hand and would send it in by email. Instead, he said: "She didn't apply."

Carol is a woman in her forties. She was doing extremely well academically on her Access course, had good support from her tutors and her family, and had thought carefully about the degree she wished to pursue. Yet at the final moment, she turned back. As her referee described it, Carol had looked again at the university website and thought: 'They're *never* going to take me – *that place* isn't for the likes of me.' In the pause over the phone line, he said: "She regrets it – is it too late?"

Carol looked dazed when she came in for interview a couple of weeks later, and laughed as she recounted her story of not applying for the course for which she was now being interviewed. She is the kind of student who has made such a difference to her programme – asking perspicacious questions from the start, taking nothing for granted – that it is hard now to imagine it without her. But her story often comes to our minds in any admissions cycle. How many potential students are there who come this close to applying to university, but draw back, and thus exclude themselves, for a variety of reasons? And if this was true for a potential applicant who was already in formal study, who else isn't looking and assumes they could never pursue a route into higher education? By their very nature, these are impossible questions to answer, since most potential applicants in this position leave no trace in the system. We were lucky, in this instance, that the applicant forgot to tell her referee that she had decided not to apply. But it is worth remembering that some 'false negatives' occur long before the process of admission even gets started.

This chapter is thus also about luck. There is a good argument that luck – social, economic, circumstantial – is a key element in the process by which students gain admission to universities. Many of the efforts to widen participation work from an assumption that we can compensate for the factors that make a student less likely to apply, or 'win' admission to, a particular university. It thus implies that it is possible to reach a stage where gaining a place at university, including at 'elite' institutions, can be entirely down to individual merit rather than privilege. In a recent study of race and admissions at elite universities in the UK and US, *The Diversity Bargain* (2016), Natasha Warikoo concludes with a thought experiment, suggesting that we should replace the current admissions system with a lottery. One reason Warikoo makes this argument is to foreground luck as an element of the process: 'A lottery would force us all – admitted students, rejected students, parents, university faculty and administrators, and society as a whole – to rethink our faith in meritocracy, and the inequality it inevitably produces' (p 201). Interestingly, something like Warikoo's lottery is held in France for admission to some of the most oversubscribed courses, such as sports courses, psychology and law, as we discuss later in this chapter.

Every way we might select large numbers of students from even larger numbers of applicants will have false positives and false negatives – there's just no way to accurately select all and only those who will do best at university, even if you know what you mean by 'doing best' (but more on that too later). Interview each student for a week, and still you can't be completely certain that they'll cope, that this is right for them at this time. And, of course, we tolerate such systems when we feel the false positive rates and false negative rates are small enough, and when we know we can't do any better. So, on its own, a single potential false negative – for example, either of the students cited so far in this chapter – shows little. But these cases are not isolated. Every year, we admit around 27 students on to the Foundation Year; 90% have no A-Levels. And there are very similar programmes at other universities in the UK, including Liverpool, Leeds, Sheffield and Birkbeck. The Open University, meanwhile, has been accepting applicants in an 'open' system, regardless of prior qualifications, for more than 50 years.

There are also comparable initiatives in other contexts. Bard College in the US runs the Bard Prison Initiative (BPI), which began as a student project in 2001, offering degrees to incarcerated men and women across New York State. More recently, Bard has started to offer 'microcolleges' in local community settings, such as libraries. One aim in both contexts is to rethink admissions, by situating the university elsewhere, and to make it accessible to those without conventional qualifications. As Max Kenner, the founder of BPI, describes it:

"We don't look at college transcripts. We don't look at college boards. We don't look at high school report cards or grades or marks or any of that stuff but we do have everyone show us a piece of writing that they've written in person, on the spot, in response to something we've provided and we do have a discussion with them."[10]

The BPI has faced considerable scepticism. Yet it made headlines in 2015, when its debate team beat Harvard College Debating Union (see Hetter, 2015). Kenner notes that the reaction to this event was revealing:

"The work we do in college in prison is always to some degree controversial. There's always a critical mass of people who think what we do is wrong, in an ethical or moral way. And what we learned from the Harvard debate was that so often when we talk about being inclusive in American higher education, or really anywhere in

American lives, people jump to the conclusion that we're lowering standards. Very often we talk about something like college being free and people assume that students who are benefitting from affordable or free education aren't earning it. It's some kind of handout, right? The Harvard event turned that on its head....

We have students who are starting at a different place but they catch up very quickly so in a lot of ways we're very conservative pedagogically. We're conservative in that we want our students to be as ambitious as possible and we hold them to very high, and reasonably objective, standards in the classroom and they do very well. They graduate from college and they get out of prison. They go to graduate schools like Columbia, Yale and NYU, top universities of the United States. So I think we have built an institution which is completely counterintuitive in the American context, almost paradoxical, which is radical in its inclusiveness but conservative in its approach to these questions of standards and of rigour."

One of the reasons Kenner describes the institution as conservative is that it insists on making a liberal arts education – history, literature, philosophy, and so on – available in these settings, whereas the pressure of public policy tends towards more prescriptive or vocational education for incarcerated people. The BPI has awarded 550 degrees and more than 50,000 credits since it started.[11]

Again, of course, an objector might reply: 'Sure – it's bad that some people miss out! We all want to teach good students who have gained their place on merit. None of us want our students' places at university to be contingent on the good fortune of their life so far. It's good that there are exceptions, like BPI and your foundation year. But we still need a system for everybody else, for the mainstream. And what else is there for them? We need to know who will cope with the material at university level, who is prepared for its rigour and complexity, and who isn't. A-Level entry requirements may be an imperfect indicator of these things, but they are nonetheless an indicator. Without an alternative, we'll have to stick with them.' But do we really lack alternatives? What are the feasible ways to reduce the false negatives in our system?

In this chapter, we explore the possibilities. We'll start by looking to the system we used in the foundation year, and we'll note some potential worries that arise if we start trying to scale it up. We'll then work through an alternative that is more scalable and hopefully still fairer than the current system. It involves combining and extending practices that already exist in the sector. We'll then end with a more radical proposal in which we propose to make access to higher education completely open. This is where our hearts lie, and that is what we have included in the list of proposals we presented in Chapter 1. However, there are loose threads within it that only further empirical research can address.

On the foundation year, we make a priority of students who don't already have a qualification at QCA Level 3 (the level at which A-Levels or an Access course sit), and who are thus not already in a position to gain a place at university through the standard routes. We decide whom to admit on the basis of a 30-minute interview and a piece of writing that we ask applicants to complete beforehand. (We include the written work assignment from the 2017 admissions period in the Appendix.) In the interview, we talk to applicants about their experience of education so far, why this is the right time for them to pursue a university education; we ask about the piece of writing they've submitted in advance, what it was like to write it, the ideas they explore in it; and we talk through how the course might fit into their life. You might expect, then, that we will propose rolling this out across the board. But there is an important sense in which initiatives of this kind work (in part) because they are relatively small scale. As Kenner notes:

"I think what we do well is create models at small scale that show how much better things can be and that's what we know how to do. We, Bard, are a small institution and BPI are a much smaller one within it and we have some degree of faith that one of the reasons why our students do so well is because the school operates at a human scale."

So what are the challenges in 'scaling up' a model of this kind? The first problem is just the amount of work involved, though as we shall see that is not quite insurmountable. For the foundation year, we typically receive 60-80 applications for a maximum of 30 places. Between three programme directors and specialist members of the recruitment team in the university, we can interview them all over a busy but manageable fortnight. But we interview only the equivalent of two or two-and-a-half people for each place, and on a small course with a high ratio of staff to students. In the wider university, there are between three and 10 applicants per place; and there are usually between 10 to 25 places per member of teaching staff. To run a robust interview process, you need two members of staff per interview – one academic and one from a specialist recruitment team. So each pair would interview between 30 and 250 would-be students – lower for courses with higher ratios of applicant to places and staff to students; higher for courses with more applicants per place and more students per member of staff. That would take between 15 and 125 hours just for the interviews alone. We need to add half as much again for reading the written work in advance of the interview, and add in time for breaks and discussion, because a tired interview team tends to make more conservative decisions. You're looking at between half a week's work and four weeks' work on admissions alone. At the lower end, these numbers are not very high, and only at the top end do they stretch beyond the realm of the possible. The admissions process at Oxford or Cambridge, where interviews are the norm, lies in the middle of this range. If such a system worked, universities might think themselves justified in replicating it across all of their degree programmes in the name of a fairer system. Of course, these figures are based on current levels of participation, and one of the goals of the system we propose in this book is to include a greater proportion of the population in higher education. If participation increased from around 50% to 90%, for instance, the amount of time spent on admissions would increase to between one week and seven weeks.

Another problem is that we currently lack robust evidence for the reliability of interviews in this context. The evidence from research on job interviews is heartening (see Conway et al, 1995). It shows that they are more reliable than psychometric and aptitude tests, at least under certain circumstances. But there is a legitimate worry that job interviews are rather different from what we are proposing, since they often happen only after an initial selection based on prior qualifications. Also, as is now gospel in human resources departments around the world, the research suggests that interviews are more reliable the more structured they are, including the same or similar questions for all candidates, rather than allowing a completely open-ended, wide-ranging discussion. We followed that practice in the foundation year interviews, but it has its limitations. As we shall see in the example of Cara below, there are applicants who perform poorly in response to the questions we use for all candidates, but open up and shine if there is room for spontaneity.

Our first proposed admissions model, therefore, does not advocate abandoning prior qualifications completely, but instead proposes a hybrid. A-Level results – or other formal qualifications, such as GCSEs, AS Levels, diplomas, Access courses, BTECs – might still play a role in this first system. But the role is changed. First, where it is possible to extract the information we need from formal qualifications, we do and we do so in the fairest way possible using what the jargon currently refers to as 'contextual offers'. Second, where that information is absent or too unreliable, we propose interviews (defined fairly broadly: this could include a whole range of face-to-face formats, tailored for particular disciplines).

Let's expand on this a little, but first a disclaimer. For the sake of making concrete proposals, we will be quite specific in what follows. But much will have to be tweaked in the light of empirical evidence that isn't currently available; and it will have to be tailored differently to different universities. We hope that the basic structure is correct: contextual offers where that makes sense, and interviews where they are required. But the cut-off between the two methods is up for grabs on the basis of what is feasible and what works. What we lay down here are principles for thinking through the method. After we've done that, we build on some of the ideas we've explored in order to imagine a, second, wholly different system.

It's worth saying as well that, structurally, this first 'mixed' method for admissions that we are proposing is not uncommon in universities now. In our own, nearly all students are admitted based on the advertised A-Level requirements or equivalent, but we also make some contextual offers, and we interview mature students. What we propose here includes the same components; but it would distribute applications to those various components in a radically different way. More students would be interviewed, and dramatically more would receive contextual offers, which would themselves span a far wider range than they currently do.

Contextual offers – using the evidence we have

Let's turn first to contextual offers. Prior results are currently used as an indicator of what is often call a student's 'academic potential'. But what exactly does this mean? Well, it could mean at least two things: a student's potential to *achieve* or *succeed* or *excel* academically, or their potential to *gain* or *grow* or *benefit* academically. The first looks just at the end of their journey – the grades they secure by the time they complete their course of study – while the second looks at the distance they've traversed during that journey – how their academic achievements have increased during their time at university; how they have grown. In the current system, when contextual offers are made, they are justified by pointing to empirical evidence that demonstrates that A-Level results on their own do not predict a student's final academic grade on their degree as reliably as A-Level results paired with certain other facts about a candidate – the sort of school they attended, the neighbourhood in which they grew up, whether or not they are the first member of their family to go to university, and so on. Students with the same A-Level results are, for instance, more likely to achieve a first-class degree – the top classification possible – if they attended a state school than if they attended an independent school.[12] The explanation? Getting a particular grade in a state school – where there's less money around, more pupils in the classrooms, and potentially more disruption from bad behaviour – demands greater ability; and that greater ability translates into a higher final grade at university. A study in 2013-14 by the Higher Education Funding Council for England (HEFCE, 2015) showed that, taking all universities and all schools together, students from state schools with ACC were only slightly less likely to obtain a first-class or upper second-class degree than those from independent schools with AAC, while state schools students with BBB were more likely to achieve this (p 22). But state schools are a heterogeneous lot, as are independent schools and universities. And more fine-grained studies suggest that the advantage given by attending an independent school increases significantly with the fees, while others suggest that whether a particular state school is achieving above or below the national average is an important factor (see Smith and Naylor 2004). So we need an admissions policy that is equally fine-grained.

This suggests a natural, evidence-based method by which an institution might set its contextual offers. Suppose your entry requirement for a student from an independent school is AAB (two A grades at A-Level and one B grade). Then you first look at how likely such a student is to achieve an upper second-class or first-class degree. Let's say 75% of independent school students with those grades obtain a degree at this level. Now, recognising the heterogeneity of state schools, you group them together into different categories, perhaps by their average A-Level results. Then, given one of these categories, you want to find the grades that a student from that group of state schools needs in order to have the same chance of obtaining an upper second-class or first-class degree. Perhaps it's BBC – that is, 75% of students from that group of state schools with two B grades and one C grade at A-Level obtain an upper second-class or first-class degree. If so, your contextual offer is BBC for students from that category of state schools.

At least, that's a common way to frame contextual offers. But we might reframe it as follows. First, find the category of state schools whose students typically achieve the average (median) A-Level results across all schools in the country, state and independent. Next, find the grades that ensure that a student coming from one of those schools with those grades has a 75% chance of achieving a first-class or an upper second-class degree. Suppose they are BBC. Then your standard offer is BBC, and your contextual offer to students from another category of school is whatever grades are required from that school to ensure a 75% chance of achieving a first class or upper second-class degree. By doing this, we stop casting independent schools as the norm – which, statistically, they are not, teaching only 7% of all pupils in the UK and 18% of all pupils over 16. We cast the average schools as the norm, and we cast the independent school students as having had an advantage over the norm. Note the parallels, for instance, between this and the recent drive to recast the disparity between treatment of men and women as male privilege, and the disparity between treatment of White and people of colour as White privilege.

So this is how universities often think about contextual offers: we look at prior results and we try to divine what final degree our applicants are likely to achieve as undergraduates. We want to admit students with the same chance of a first-class degree, the same chance of an upper second, a lower second, and so on. This was made very explicit in Cambridge University's spat with the UK government over the predictive power of AS-Level grades and GCSE grades. When the government threatened to remove AS-Levels from the high school curriculum, Cambridge asked that they should remain, arguing that their analysis showed that a student's AS-Level grades better predict their final degree performance than GCSE grades do.[13]

But notice this: while the intentions behind these contextual offers are on the side of the angels, they still put many students at a disadvantage. The problem lies in the goal that we set for an admissions procedure, namely, the goal of highest average degree classification among graduating students. Having set this goal, we run studies to determine how to make contextual offers to best achieve it. But these studies count for little if the goal is the wrong one. And we argue that it is.

The goal favours potential to *achieve* over potential to *benefit*. And these are quite different goals. What's more, admissions policies that serve one do not necessarily serve the other. Now, it's no great surprise that intellectual achievement rather than intellectual growth has been the goal of universities. For one thing, it is enshrined in the league table system, which drives much thinking at the top levels of universities. University league tables – often published by media outlets such as *Times Higher Education*, *The Guardian* and *The Telegraph* – are a wide and varied menagerie. But, on each, a university's position is determined in part by the percentage of first-class, upper second-class and lower second-class degrees awarded to graduates. So that's a practical motivation. But there is an ideological one as well. Among many academics at some of the most prestigious universities in the UK, there is a feeling that there is a significant division between secondary and tertiary education that does not exist between primary and secondary education. They suggest that primary and secondary schools, not universities, bear the responsibility for ironing out any discrepancies in academic performance that arise from social background. In an ideal world, they seem to suggest, the primary and secondary school system would deliver students to the university admissions with the same level of preparation, regardless of their history. And in that world, universities would be free to focus solely on bringing them to the highest possible level for their final exams – when the starting point is the same, final achievement and benefit obtained coincide. Here's Mary Beard, a professor of Classics at Cambridge University:

> One of the problems we've identified in my college is that people have made wrong A-level choices, so we're now putting a lot of effort into Year 11 kids to help them make good choices. (Cited in Rustin, 2011)

Ian Philips (2016), a professor of philosophy at the University of Birmingham, who used to be involved in the admissions process at the University of Oxford, does acknowledge the pressures that the current system places on applicants, although he still seems to conceive this largely as the student's responsibility:

> Because interviews are scary it does require you, as a 17-year-old, to really back yourself and get on the train down from wherever to come here. It is a kind of a big thing to do and if you're discouraged then it could be easy for that to have a big impact.

Such academics may be right – about that ideal world that they envisage, at least. But that is not the world we inhabit, nor is it anywhere near to being realised. So conclusions about it cannot be transported without question to the world we do inhabit. Since even Cambridge can only reach into a small proportion of schools in the country, and since many 15-year-olds will remain woefully unaware of what different university courses might involve, might they not direct their efforts towards taking students who would benefit most from university regardless of which A-Levels they choose to pursue? And might they not expend some of that energy speaking not only to schools, but to community organisations, employers and libraries, to attract those who left school some time ago? Is Oxford doing all it can to make the interview process less 'scary', more welcoming, more inclusive? Need the interviews take place in Oxford, rather than in the students' hometowns? Need they take the form of traditional interviews – crammed into 30 intense, mind-scrambling minutes of impostor syndrome and self-doubt, rather than group exercises, discussion groups, and so on? How much more difficult is it to 'back yourself' at the age of 17 when few people have ever backed you before?

The goal, we argue, should not be potential to achieve but potential to benefit. Think of Jake and Abbi. Jake is 19 and he's applying to university with three A-Levels at grade B. There were few bumps in the road as Jake worked through high school. His parents are present and they're supportive; he didn't get ill, didn't suffer a bereavement, attended a state school with a very middle-class intake; Jake is White, he's straight, and he's a cis man – he hasn't had to come out about his gender or his sexuality at high school; he's never had to cope with the drip-drip of casual homophobia, nor been abused because of his ethnicity, nor been side-lined in a physics class because he's a woman. Abbi's 49. She left school at 18 with one A-Level at grade C, and a mixed bag of GCSEs, having spent her final school years in and out of hospital with anorexia; she tried to return to study for A-Levels at college when she had recovered, but she was socially isolated, she was short of money, and she needed to work; in her mid-twenties she had two sons, who have been promising to leave home for four years, but never seem to manage it. Abbi is a Black British woman, her school sent very few pupils to university, and she will be the first from her family to go. Jake gets a high upper second for his degree, averaging 68, putting him in the top fifth of students at his university, while Abbi graduates with a high lower second, averaging 58, meaning that three out of five of her classmates will graduate with higher grades. With little background knowledge of universities and the way they work, Abbi found it difficult to navigate the institution, while Jake found it easy; she was reluctant to ask for help, while Jake was not; as she sat in the induction event on her first day, looking around at the vast oak-panelled room where she was gathered with her new classmates, she looked at the portraits around the hall of previous vice-chancellors of the university – every last one of them an older White man – and she never shook off the feeling that this place wasn't for her.

If our goal is to maximise the degree classification that our students, on average, achieve, Jake is a better bet than Abbi. We know that Black British students perform less well in final university exams than their White classmates who entered with the same A-Level results and from the same educational backgrounds.[14] The challenges that arise from being black in an educational setting that is almost exclusively White – from the senior management to the academic and professional staff to the scholars you learn about and the classmates you study with – are significant. Having children also has an impact – their demands on your time don't let up just because you've enrolled at university. And being an older student surrounded by classmates in their late teens – that takes its toll as well. So, in a sense, Abbi's final results were reasonably predictable from the outset, and are reliant on certain kinds of luck, much as with the admissions system. And a university set on maximising those final results would have thought her a bad bet. This is exacerbated by the fact that Abbi might also be less likely to complete her degree, and thus to be classed as an 'unsuccessful leaver', as was Simon (whose story we considered in Chapter 3).

'Value added' – this term seems to have migrated into the jargon of education management. It is often still used to refer to the economic or monetary value that was its original meaning in the business world. But there is a distinctive sort of value that education can add to a person's life – it isn't reducible to their employability or earning power or contribution to the national economy, but it's real all the same; it's the sort of value we discussed in Chapter 4. And, if we read 'value' in that way, the term 'value added' does capture what universities should aim to provide. We should aim to admit students for whom we can add most of this value. Abbi's journey, for instance, covered much more ground than Jake's; her university experience added more – from C at A-Level to a lower second-class degree is further than from BBB to an upper second. It is this goal we should be aiming for when we make contextual offers. Indeed, it raises a related question about what measures we use to classify a degree at its end and when an individual's studies are 'complete'. If we abolish the degree structure, as we have proposed, and replace it with a transcript of modules completed, Abbi's achievements could be judged more clearly on their own merits, rather than as belonging to one category rather than another, on which she missed out by two marks.

All of the existing empirical work tells us how to make contextual offers when our goal is to maximise achievement rather than gain. So the sorts of offers we propose to make require new empirical data. We need to know which combinations of prior results, school background, and other characteristics such as ethnicity, socioeconomic level and so on, give the highest chance of high value added.

Interviews, written work, preparatory courses: excavating for new evidence

Now, there will still be some for whom contextual offers will not help. Among those applying to the foundation year, 90% had no A-Levels at all – some were refugees from countries where schooling wasn't available, others had struggled with addiction or homelessness in their teenage years – and others had gained the results they did have under such idiosyncratic conditions that those results would be a poor predictor of their abilities – they suffered severe mental or physical health, cared for sick parents or became parents themselves during their time at high school. The same will be true of the applicants to a university model of the kind we propose, and it is already true for a large number of those who complete qualifications at the Open University. One option for these applicants would be interviews. The numbers will be smaller and interviews thus more manageable.

Another option would be written work. When we were selecting students for the foundation year, we drew on personal statements from the candidates, references from someone who could speak for them, 30-minute interviews, and a three- or four-page piece of written work that we set in advance. The Bard Prison Initiative uses a similar strategy. Written work allows us to see how a person's mind works when it has greater time and space to ponder a question, to interact with a poem or a photograph or a film, to analyse their own reactions and put together an argument or an interpretation. Interviews give something complementary – they allow a two-way exchange; they allow us to probe parts of the written work that are unclear, or where it seems that a deeper insight has been left unspoken or unexplored; it allows us to liberate ideas that may have become rather trapped in the process of writing them, giving applicants confidence in an insight and seeing how they build on that; they allow us to talk about the demands of university education, how the applicant might meet them, how they view that education. In short, they give us a strong sense of the added value that might be achieved for this student, in the sense discussed earlier – and that's what we're looking for.

Earlier in this chapter, in the context of the Oxbridge admissions procedure, we noted that interviews come with their own problems. People get stage fright; they clam up. Impostor syndrome strikes and they give monosyllabic answers, or the answers they imagine the interviewers want to hear. While our institution is not as imposing or intimidating as an Oxbridge college, when someone arrives for the first time, often with no prior experience of the university, it can have a profound effect on them.

Cara was 34 when she arrived at the entrance to the Woodland Road building, described at the start of Chapter 3, to be interviewed for the foundation year. It was an unseasonably hot day in March, and I was interviewing in a colleague's office at the top of the building that houses the English department. It seemed to be collecting all of the heat from elsewhere in the building, and even with the window open, the air felt stagnant. I knew from Cara's application form that she hoped to progress from the foundation year to a degree in English, so I mentioned that where we were now would be her home department. I don't think this helped. The office was the archetype of a don's lair. Every inch of the desk piled high with papers and books, the floor doubling as further desk space, the walls hung with reproductions of etchings. For some, that can seem enticing – finally entering the sort of space you've imagined and yearned for, but from which you've always been excluded. Not for Cara. For her, the setting added to a sense that this was all too much; that the distance she had to travel from where she was now to where this office suggested was simply too far.

The start of the interview proceeded as if she had made up her mind already that she had made a mistake. She seemed to want the experience over as quickly as possible. Her answers were brief, and when I asked about her interest in literature, there was no flicker of enthusiasm, no suggestion that it would excite her to study poetry or plays or prose for three years. Yet all of this was at odds with her written work – a treatment of a Seamus Heaney poem – and her personal statement, which was articulate and committed. I half-wondered whether a friend or a relative had written them; this had happened before and has happened since.

I was beginning to share Cara's hope that the interview would end soon when I remembered a striking aspect of the application: Cara was a performance poet; she wrote and performed spoken word pieces. So I asked her about that. Her face changed completely. She started telling me where she'd performed most recently, and where she was performing next. It was all just factual information, but at least she was talking. Then she stopped. She paused, clearly weighing in her mind whether or not to say something. After a moment, she asked: "Do you want to hear one?" Of course I did. What followed was extraordinary. For five minutes, she performed entirely from memory a complex, brilliant piece of poetry, laying the emphasis with such precision on specific syllables, sometimes to create the pulse of the verse, sometimes to jolt the listener into paying attention to an unusual choice of words. It was like she was lost in a trance as she did it, her concentration was so total. She finished, I applauded, and we started to talk about the process of writing it. She explained how she'd chosen the topic, the rhythm, the words; she talked about editing it, practising it, and finally performing it. And soon we were on to the Heaney poem she had read for the written work. She was talking as a poet herself. Why would he have chosen those words? Why choose to reveal that detail at that point? When he pushed those two memories together into one poem, was he driven only by making a political point, or did that pairing just appeal to him, aesthetically? The transformation was total.

Before we interview each year, I often think about that experience, and I wonder what would have happened had we not hit on the topic of Cara's spoken-word activities. Would she have been another false negative even of a system designed to find her? My memory of her spoken word performances came unbidden. It easily might not have – luck, again.

For interviews to be done well, then, there must be space for dialogue. Those running them must be trained. They must know the empirical research we described earlier – greater structure makes for greater reliability. But they must also know how to give interviewees the best possible hearing, how to elicit the very best from them. Having two interviewers usually helps as well; the interview with Cara was unusual in our practice because I interviewed her on my own. Of course, if the rest of the system changes as we envisage, and the university becomes a more central part of the life of the community around it, it should itself become less intimidating.

Interviewers must be aware how the university environment intimidates and silences those who have historically been excluded from it, and they must be able to create as safe a space for those people as possible. But they must also be trained in what to look for. We have a tendency to judge a person's aptitude for a task by measuring how closely they resemble the prototype we store in our imagination of someone who is good at that task (see Kahneman and Tversky, 1972; Blair et al, 2001; Bordalo et al, 2016). That prototype is in turn formed by looking at the status quo. This is part of what gives rise to stereotyping. If interviews are going to aid inclusion, those who conduct them must be trained to resist this tendency.

Open access

We now turn to our second, more radical, proposed admissions model. This proposal moves beyond our current model of higher education, and imagines what admissions might look like in a university system that has been transformed along the lines we have proposed in earlier chapters. This is a university in which a module has become the key unit; in which the first 60 credits any learner takes are offered for free; and in which the final 'qualification' a student achieves is in the form of an evolving transcript of their results – thus showing, for example, variation and improvement rather than just an overall mark. What might admissions look like now?

The former extra-mural departments, the Open University, and the non-selective French *université* system that is currently under threat offer one way of managing admission to the first 60 credits of learning: these initial modules would be *entirely open access* – that is, anyone could enrol, for free, regardless of prior qualifications.[15] In fact, our proposal would be that the 60-credit entitlement might be an entitlement to 60 *successful* credits, with space for up to 40 credits that the student does not complete. This would also allow scope for students sometimes to undertake a module and choose not to take the assessment, though not an unlimited number of times.

There would be no time limit on this offer of free, open access learning – it would come with no expiry date. Our system of shorter modules would deliberately allow students multiple chances to engage with higher education. So, someone might take a 20-credit module, and then return 10 or 20 years later to take two more modules of that kind. Or, someone might fail a module the first time but still be entitled to return and take other units, having learned more about what suits and stimulates them.

Beyond the initial 60 credits, students' engagement with their studies would be on a different basis because at that point they would start to pay a participatory education tax. We propose that this is the point at which a student could indicate a specialism, but would not have to do so. So there would be two routes from this stage onwards, as follows:

- **Access to some routes beyond initial study would be completely open.** On this 'generalist' route, students who had completed 60 credits could continue without additional prior qualifications. Some modules beyond this point might have particular prerequisites – if you want to take Advanced Topics in Evolutionary Theory, you'll have to first have taken Introduction to Evolution, for instance – and a small number would be reserved for students pursuing a particular specialism. But the assumption would be that modules should be open to all wherever possible; modules reserved for a specialism would be the exception, and a case would have to be made to run a module that way.

- **Access to specialist routes beyond initial study would be fairer.** There would continue to be a limited number of 'specialist' routes through subsequent study, for example where a particular route might be required for a profession such as medicine, social work or the law. This route would have an admissions procedure, which could take account of achievement in the 60 credits already completed at university as well as either prior achievement in another qualification (such as A-Levels or an Access course), in which contextual data would be applied, or written work and interview, tailored for the subject area. This would allow for a clear system in which prior qualifications could be either acknowledged or disregarded.

Is such a system feasible? One concern is oversubscription.[16] How should we control the demand for places on courses, particularly for some of the most popular courses at some of the most prestigious institutions, which are likely to retain their popularity and prestige even after the overhaul we propose here? There are broadly two styles of response: the first is followed in the French *université* system; the second is the Open University's strategy, features of which were also adopted by the former extramural departments. We propose a hybrid of the two.

The French system is a central planning system. Each year, would-be students submit an ordering of the courses they'd like to pursue together with the universities at which they'd like to study them. Places on these courses are then allocated centrally by the French government with an eye to giving as many students as possible places on the courses that they ranked highly. When a course is oversubscribed, however – as is often the case for degrees in sports studies, psychology and law – without any recourse to the students' prior results, the system chooses almost at random, giving some weighting to those who wish to attend their local university.

The Open University manages demand differently. Instead of a central planning model, it is a market-based model – as demand increases, the institution supplies more. It can do this partly because it does not have a physical campus, so that increasing its numbers doesn't place a strain on lecture theatre space and decreasing them doesn't leave rooms empty. Also, much of its teaching is carried out remotely by tutors on flexible contract; this was also the case with the extra-mural departments, which also contracted tutors in response to demand for the courses they provided. Furthermore, it makes use of distance-learning methods, such as online teaching. Also, as a less prestigious institution, demand for its courses has never been the same as that for Oxford or Cambridge, which would most likely remain in our model. So, again, we face the problem of scaling up a solution that works at the small scale and in part because it is the exception rather than the norm.

Nearly all universities in the UK have physical campuses, and some are in high demand, either because of the prestige of studying there – which might reflect the quality of the teaching students receive, the research undertaken there, or the esteem in which employers hold the degrees they award – or because the city in which they are based is attractive. Also, while the flexibility offered by teaching contracts at the Open University works well while that is a single institution among others with a more traditional structure, there are already worries about the casualisation of teaching labour in higher education, and we would not want this to become a structural feature across the sector. It is important to remember that flexible contracts are sometimes desirable for employees as well as employers, and so a reasonable supply of such contracts does little harm; but it is also crucial to acknowledge the problems that arise when casualisation becomes the norm, as it might when a non-selective system means that the number of places an institution must provide on its various different degree programmes are not as stable as they are now.

However, there are equally problems with a model that relies entirely on central planning. In the French system, a student whose passion is psychology, and who has a natural aptitude for the subject, might end up assigned to a degree in physics. So, while we will borrow from the French system and propose to use a lottery when demand is too high, with a weighting in favour of those who wish to study locally, at least for the first 60 credits worth of learning, we also borrow from the Open University a blended model of study that combines in-person and online learning and assessment. By doing this, we expand a university's capacity to teach much larger numbers of students.

False negatives are the people our admissions system fails; the people wrongly excluded from higher education, not because they would not be able to cope with it, nor because they wouldn't benefit from it, but because the admissions system is not designed to include them. They are the people we met on the foundation year – countless people who would have been false negatives but for that course. Ashley, an 18-year-old who suffered from bulimia during their school years and couldn't sit the exams; Brian, who has suffered from bipolar disorder since he was 12, who sat his exams but performed well below his ability; Violet, a social worker her whole adult life, a mother and grandmother, who was led to believe that university was not for the likes of her, holding a stock of O-Levels and nursing qualifications, but no A-Levels; Nira, who left school at 16 after falling out with her parents and who has cared for her disabled son for the past 10 years; David, who has been in the Royal Air Force for the past 20 years and wants to retrain; these, and over 100 other students on the foundation year and 150 more on the BA in English Literature and Community Engagement. When you raise concerns with our current admissions system – when you raise the spectre of these hundreds and thousands of false negatives – its defenders are wont to point out that you can only guarantee that there will be no false negatives in a system if you admit everyone. It is precisely such a system that we have arrived at in this chapter.

6

The women in Plato's Academy

In brief, the argument of this book is simply this: the current system excludes people from a university education unfairly, and at the points in their lives when they might most need it, or want it, or when they would benefit from it most. In contrast, our proposed system includes those who would benefit, and it includes them on a schedule of their choosing. If we give arguments for our proposal beyond this, there is a danger that we concede too much to the status quo. When someone gives extra arguments for a view that they hold, arguments beyond their central motivating argument, it can sometimes suggest to their audience that those arguments are necessary to establish it; they suggest that their central argument doesn't succeed on its own – as the philosopher Anthony Flew puts it in *God and Philosophy*, 'if one leaky bucket will not hold water, there is no reason to think that ten can.' Nevertheless, acknowledging that risk, we make some further positive arguments for our proposal here. What's more, there are certain sorts of argument against which we'd like to defend our proposal, so we take up a few sceptical perspectives here as well.

"People in this country have had enough of experts."

This was Michael Gove, then justice secretary, campaigning for Brexit. Unable to name a single economist who viewed the UK's prospective exit from the UK with enthusiasm, Gove lashed out at all experts indiscriminately. His words were heard by those who disagreed as the epitome of post-truth politics, where politicians pay scant attention to arguments or evidence or any of those things we typically look to when we want a reliable guide to the truth. But there is another way to hear what Gove said, and we suspect it is closer to what he intended and closer to how it was heard by those he was primarily addressing. People in this country have had enough of being told what to do and what to think by people whose methods and terminology are mysterious to them; where the means by which those people come to their conclusions are opaque or outlandishly complex; and where these barriers of language and method, not dissimilar to those we explored within universities in Chapter 3, make it impossible for a lay person to participate or contribute on equal terms.[17] These people who tell us what to do and what to think are 'boffins', and while many of us trust the boffins who build our aircraft or MRI machines, since their track record of success is relatively plain to see and there is nothing overtly political about what they tell us, the social sciences and economics in particular have a more equivocal scorecard and are highly politicised. Now, part of the reason why these methods seem so remote and why the experts who use them are not trusted is that they are not within the social experience of Gove's intended audience. While those who voted for Brexit had a wide variety of reasons for doing so, they tended to be older, and they tended not to have studied at university. Thus, their contact with the sort of expertise that Michael Gove decried – which has its roots strongly in universities, if not only there – was either distant or simply did not exist.

If we're right, one part of the way to change this situation is to ensure that a much wider range of people participate in higher education across the full course of their life. This would go some way to demystifying experts and the expertise to which they act as guardians and stewards, including as the expertise itself changes in response to societal and technological developments. There are compelling arguments for the public benefits of universities as they stand: the fact that research on diseases any of us may experience, for example, happens within universities. But it is one thing to be told about an abstract public benefit. It is very different to be able to witness, or participate in, its creation or question its premise on equal terms, as is possible in the seminar room or laboratory. Experts are, after all, just ordinary people. They are people who have spent a lot of time learning, using and developing methods that seek to divine the truth in their particular subject, whether that is a prediction about the economy or the Higgs boson particle, an interpretation of a poem or a historical text, a solution to a philosophical or mathematical puzzle, or the aetiology of a particular illness. They are no different from car mechanics, pilots, electricians, doctors, or hair stylists. But those latter we encounter in our daily lives, and so their expertise is less remote, and we may feel more able to enter into dialogue about what these experts tell us, or to trust it because we have seen it operate with our own eyes. As things stand, and as E.P. Thompson articulated it, expertise within universities is currently tested against too narrow a range of experiences, which has consequences for the knowledge that experts produce as well.

While the methods of these experts may look mysterious and dizzyingly complex to those who haven't learned to use them, they are simply the result of many people over many years trying to figure out how the world works, and trying to develop ways to coax the world into giving up its secrets. Statistics, for instance, one of the least trusted areas of expertise, is not some esoteric topic with an exotic subject matter – correlation coefficients, statistical significance, the power of a test. It is just a well-developed theory of how to reason reliably from the sort of evidence we typically have about what will happen in complex systems like the human body, an economic market, or a social movement. We all have experience of how to move from evidence to practice, albeit on a different scale: for example, we may be cautious when crossing a particular road as a pedestrian, because we know there have been several accidents there, from reports in the local paper or from other parents in our child's school. In this situation, we are responding to statistical evidence and altering our behaviour in a complex traffic system (which already requires our constant evaluation of situations and evidence) on the basis of it. As Raymond Williams (1961) argued:

> There are no ordinary activities, if by 'ordinary' we mean the absence of creative interpretation and effort. Everything we see and do, the whole structure of our relationships and institutions, depends, finally, on an effort of learning, description and communication. (p 34)

So the subjects themselves may not be mysterious, but their connections to apparently 'ordinary' human activities have been obscured. Familiarity with them is what is needed, as well as an opportunity to participate in the creation of evidence, rather than just to experience its effects. This is what we aim to ensure in the remade model of universities that we propose. This would not lead to a magical future in which we all agree with one another. Quite the opposite: what it *could* point towards, as Mwenza Blell articulated it in Chapter 3, is a more realistic utopia – a society in which we are able to hear one another, disagree and live with the consequences.

In our model, universities weave expertise, scholarship, critical thinking and learning collaboratively into our everyday lives, and, if we so choose, throughout the whole course of our lives. In this model, the experts who inform the policy decisions that affect our lives are also the lecturers who pass on their knowledge to us in their classes; they are the people who lead our seminars, and who help us design and execute the projects that we undertake on our university courses. But our proposals go beyond this. The argument we have just given recalls the argument for public engagement. And while that is a crucial component in any institution of learning, we want to go further, not just making the experts visible to the public, but intertwining expertise and experience, blurring the boundaries, and ensuring dialogue and collaboration between them. Here's why.

"Where were the women while Plato's Academy met? Making them lunch, I'll bet."

This is Joan, a student on the foundation year, in the middle of a seminar on ancient Greek attitudes to death. It is often said that, given that nature distributes raw ability and talent with equal generosity over all social groups, increasing diversity is just good statistics. Relying on self-sufficient members of the upper classes to do science and philosophy, as we did in the 17th and 18th centuries, is inevitably going to produce less rapid progress than when our academy is populated with women, people of colour, people from middle- and working-class backgrounds, and so on. But it turns out that there is a greater advantage to inclusion than simply casting the net wider so that it includes more people of talent. The very inclusion of people from a variety of backgrounds in our discussions enhances academic work well beyond the contribution that their individual talent makes. This has long been believed in arts and humanities subjects and in the social sciences, where the problems that academics study are naturally addressed best if there are many different viewpoints present, bringing the special knowledge that those viewpoints afford. But it is true also of the sciences, as we'll see.

History, it is often said, is written by the victors. What is less often emphasised is that this is true not only of the victors in a war, but more generally of the victors in life: those who find themselves at the top of the social hierarchy; those with the education to write, the raw materials to do it, the time to spend on it, and the influence to ensure that what they set down is preserved by future generations. So when our impression of a time is based on written accounts of it, the voices preserved in them are not diverse and we need to look beyond those accounts to discover a more balanced truth. Oftentimes, it falls to a member of an excluded group to identify the absence of voices like theirs. So we have histories of the working class in large part because of working-class writers, such as Robert Tressell (pen-name of Robert Noonan, author of *The Ragged Trousered Philanthropists*) and working-class historians, and the connections between working-class members of the communist movement and middle-class historians like Christopher Hill, E.P. Thompson, Raphael Samuel and Eric Hobsbawm; we have feminist readings of literary texts because of women like Simone du Beauvoir, Kate Millett, Elaine Showalter, Hazel Carby, and bell hooks; we have a theory of intersectionality because of Kimberlé Williams Crenshaw, a Black woman working in law schools in the US, and Black feminist activists, such as the Combahee River Collective; the theory of microaggressions begins with the Black psychiatrist Chester Pierce, and is developed more fully by the Chinese American academic psychologist Derald Wing Sue; the female philosopher Miranda Fricker gave the world the concept of epistemic injustice, a way of understanding how individuals can experience injustice specifically as a 'knower', when their own knowledge is disbelieved or when they lack the concepts they need to explain it; and the female geneticist Mary-Claire King laid the groundwork for identifying the gene, BRCA1, that causes breast cancer. The list goes on and on. Now, this should come as little surprise. So much of intellectual insight arises from *noticing* something that hasn't been seen before – and what you notice is at least partly determined by what you've seen, what you've experienced, what you feel.

Of course, not all insights are born equal. Not everyone will contribute a novel view of their subject that will open up a new area of philosophy or history, as Miranda Fricker and the historians of the working class did, or identify the basis for a new treatment for breast cancer, as King's work did. But intellectual endeavour is cumulative. It benefits from the accretion of countless insights deposited over time. If the list above gives an indication of some of the achievements made possible by opening up the academy gradually and partially over the past hundred years, just imagine what might be in store should it become truly inclusive.

However, this makes it sound as if an inclusive academy only ever helps us to identify issues that affect groups that have previously been excluded: let in women and you get feminist literary criticism and better healthcare for women; let in gays, lesbians, and trans people and you have queer theory and the demographics of gender and sexuality; and so on. But this isn't true. In her inaugural lecture as a professor, our colleague Havi Carel spoke of the experience of having a chronic illness (see also Carel, 2014). There's much that it takes away, for sure, she said – pastimes, perhaps, that you once enjoyed but are now no longer possible. But she wanted to emphasise that there is much that it gives as well. And one thing it gives is a particular vantage point on the world. Having a chronic illness in a world full of relatively healthy people pulls you outside the mainstream of society. And from there you can better observe it and see its absurdities. You can see better the places where it is structured some way because of historical accident fossilised by the weight of conservatism, rather than because it is the best way for things to be. But it isn't just chronic illness that pulls you outside of society like that. Those who do not occupy a privileged position in society will often occupy a vantage point 'outside' the assumptions of society: women; people of colour; disabled and ill people; gays, lesbians, and transgender people; people who don't wish to identify with traditional genders; the members of the working class; and so on. And this vantage point will often allow them to analyse various aspects of the world that are just not salient for people for whom the current norms of society always work and who are always supported by them. Including these insights into academic life will enrich it greatly, just as the academy has improved every time its demographic has broadened.

This is all very well for the arts and humanities and the social sciences, you might think, but do the advantages of inclusion accrue in the sciences as well? It is becoming well established that they do. In science, research is more often done by groups of researchers than by the lone scholars that still dominate in arts and humanities and social science research. The group that runs the Large Hadron Collider, the world's most powerful particle accelerator at CERN, the European Organization for Nuclear Research, or the group that mapped the human genome are two of the more famous groups, but in the science, engineering and medical faculties of every university and research institute in the world, teams are working together to address a particular problem. They contribute different expertise: sometimes practical expertise – aptitude with an electron microscope, for instance – sometimes theoretical – knowledge of some special group of viruses, perhaps. The evidence suggests that these groups produce better science when they are more diverse.[18] Their papers make more of an impact, being cited by other scholars more often; they are published in more prestigious journals; they receive funding and prizes and awards more often; and so on. Why might that be? What is it about a collaboration between a diverse group of people that produces better quality work? There is less consensus here, but there are a number of plausible suggestions. Those working in diverse groups tend to feel that they must prove the quality of their contributions by backing them up with careful argument and evidence more than those in homogeneous groups, where the quality is sometimes taken for granted. As a result, they prepare better for these collaborative discussions. People from different backgrounds and different social groups have often learned different strengths – they are more socially perceptive, or more focussed, or more competitive, or more critical. Many problems will only be solved when all of these skills are brought to bear on them. Few individuals have them all; few homogeneous groups have them either. But heterogeneous groups often do.

Diversity bargains

In 1958, Michael Young wrote a dystopian fiction about a 'meritocracy', in which ideas of 'merit' would be used by the existing elite to reinforce class structures, rather than dismantling them, in part by fooling the lower classes into giving consent for a system that was still intrinsically unequal but was masked by a rhetoric of fairness. In Young's fiction: 'The top of today are breeding the top of tomorrow to a greater extent than at any time in the past' (p 175). It is an irony that Young's term has been used subsequently – including by New Labour – without its origins always being acknowledged.

Remember how we started this chapter: we acknowledged a certain danger that arises when we offer arguments for our proposal that go beyond the straightforward argument from social justice that provides the central motivation for this book – if our central argument is watertight, there is surely no need for further arguments; if it isn't, we still have work to do. At this point, we see another danger – heard independently of the argument from social justice, the arguments given here run the risk of supporting the sort of dystopian 'meritocracy' that Michael Young envisaged. On this view, women, those from minority ethnic communities, and others are accepted into the 'elite' as a series of exceptional individuals and because of what they can contribute. They are accepted because of what the elite themselves can gain from them being there – new research questions, better scholarship, a higher quality of collaborative research. This means, of course, that someone from a group that is not well represented needs to be exceptional in order to gain admittance or thrive in the system. A White man, on the other hand, can do very well by performing a little below average.

Natasha Warikoo (2016) calls this a 'diversity frame', and suggests it is key to how affirmative action is viewed at elite universities in the United States: '[Students] appreciated diversity on campus for the enrichment it brought to their own educational experience rather than for its impact on racial justice or the lives of students benefiting from affirmative action' (p 186). In contrast, Warikoo suggests, many students in the UK have a 'colour-blindness frame', thinking that merit alone should determine (for example) who is admitted to Oxbridge: 'While the two frames differ in their assumptions about the importance of race in society, they share a lack of attention to differences in power and resources between racial groups' (pp 186-7). Warikoo frames the solution partly as an educational one: students need a 'power analysis frame' and they need to learn about 'racial exclusion in American history' (p 194).

A power analysis frame is also vital for acknowledging the histories of racial and gender exclusion in the university as a workplace, and the way in which these histories are still present in the barriers faced (for example) by a Black, female colleague in entering the academy and remaining there. To do that, as Warikoo shows, neither a 'colour-blindness frame' of merit and excellence nor a 'diversity frame' in which we are all 'enriched' is adequate. We also need (at least) Warikoo's 'power analysis frame', in which we acknowledge the pain and violence and injustice of exclusion as well.

This is why it is critical to the arguments we make throughout this book that, rather than (for example) admitting a different range of individuals to the current higher education system, the system itself needs to change. Sara Ahmed (2012, p 164) writes about the challenges of entering a system as an outsider:

'Being included' can ... be to experience an increasing proximity to those norms that historically have been exclusive; the extension of the norms might be not only a fantasy but also a way of being made increasingly subject to their violence.... Diversity is often imagined as a form of repair, a way of mending or fixing histories of being broken. Indeed, diversity enters institutional discourse as a language of reparation; as a way of imagining that those who are divided can work together; as a way of assuming that 'to get along'. Not to be excluded becomes not simply an account of the present ... but also a way of relating to the past ..."

This is another frame – a 'reconciliation frame', if you like – to add to Warikoo's 'diversity' and 'colour-blindness' frames. It says that diversity is good because it allows old wounds to heal. But too often that healing process involves hiding the weapons that caused the wounds in the first place. Ahmed illustrates this with the following example:

In the book *Life in the United Kingdom*, on which British citizenship tests are based, there is one reference to slavery and that is to abolitionism. The nation is remembered as the liberator of slaves, not as the perpetrator of slavery. (2012, p 184)

Universities themselves, as Ahmed's work shows, have become experts at telling their own histories in this way, in which Black and minority ethnic staff are – in their very bodies, as used in publicity materials and similar – asked to perform the idea that the institution has become inclusive. A different starting point for all universities would be to teach their own histories critically to all students.

A lived account of 'being included' is also evident in the opening pages of bell hooks' *Teaching to Transgress*, in which she writes about a painful move she experienced as a child, from segregated Black schools to desegregated White ones:

> That shift from beloved, all-black schools to white schools where black students were always seen as interlopers, as not really belonging, taught me the difference between education as the practice of freedom and education that merely strives to reinforce domination. (2014, p 4)

So, while the benefits of an inclusive academy *for the academy* cannot be overstated, those benefits cannot furnish the sole reason for being more inclusive. If they do, the academy will inflict a heavy cost on the newly included people, for its spaces and structures, its processes and systems, its norms and modes of behaviour will continue to bear the marks of their previous exclusion.

The arguments from social justice must remain the motivating ones. Only by giving them sufficient prominence will institutions change as they come to include more people, so that they are owned and shaped equally by all and so that their norms do not exclude; so that certain individuals do not feel like interlopers and so that inclusion in the academy doesn't bring someone closer to the forms of oppression that excluded them in the first place. This is education as what Freire and hooks call the 'practice of freedom', in which the very acts of education – teaching, learning, enquiry, co-creation – are a means by which the world can be examined critically and changed.

One part of this process is to continue to 'decentre' universities, seeking to make them less hierarchical in decision making, more responsive to new individuals and experiences, and more flexible in their structures. hooks' experience shows that sometimes 'closed' communities – for women of colour, for example – can allow for conversations about the experiences of a minority that are harder to have in a larger structure, where an individual is asked to share those experiences in a way that may make them vulnerable to the very structures that have oppressed them. This is a point our own students have made about the transition from the foundation year to a degree. In the former environment, with a student body that spans a wide age range and a varied motley of experiences, there is often a willingness to share life experiences openly. In contrast, on a degree alongside 18-year-olds, one student noted: "You feel you don't want to maybe give something of yourself, your life experience or whatever, because you don't know how it's going to be received ... almost like you've given part of yourself away really and it hasn't been reciprocated" (cited in Johnson, forthcoming). For this reason, we argue that universities should make it easier for communities of knowledge to emerge within the academy, where minority experiences can be central and can still retain dialogue with wider university structures.

Imagine, for example, that in the participatory budgeting process one region identified a need for more research on the experiences of young people who were transgender, or who were considering transitioning. This is an area of highly contentious debate at present and one in which it can be difficult for trans people to feel their voices are heard and their experiences understood. One way forward might be the creation of a centre for research, practice and teaching in this area in which the majority or all of the participants initially would be trans people themselves, and in which decisions would be made collectively. The centre would retain dialogue with other parts of the university, sharing knowledge and the results of its research. Over, say, a five-year period, there would be an increasing movement of staff and students between the centre and the wider university, allowing for ideas, curricula and research projects to become shared. Ultimately, there might be discussion about whether the centre would retain its separate identity or be reformed in a different way within the larger university. If the centre served its purpose – of creating change – it might then itself be able to adapt to new circumstances.

"But what about the hard-working school pupil?"

This is a sceptical colleague during the consultation we held with teaching staff in the months leading up to the launch of the foundation year. And there will inevitably be others who say that, far from being a fairer vision of a university, opening possibilities to those currently excluded, the model we propose instead fails to sufficiently recognise and appropriately reward those who battle through at school, sometimes against the odds, sometimes overcoming extraordinary hardships to succeed. These are the prospective students who play the role in this debate that is played by 'hard-working families' in the debate on benefits or universal basic income; they are the 'deserving poor' of the higher education debate. The same language dominates each of these discussions: it's the language of desert, of hard work, of incentives to succeed and the dire consequences when those incentives are removed.

Take Stacie, for instance, a 16-year-old who has cared for a mother with Alzheimer's disease throughout her GCSEs; who fits in study in between preparing meals; and who aces her exams when they come around. Why would Stacie have tried so hard if the higher education system had been as we would like to see it, ready to take her without qualifications?

Against Stacie, of course, we might pit Robin, whose father dies in the months leading up to their A-Levels, who loses all motivation, and doesn't study at all, failing their exams or achieving grades well below their ability; or Chloe, whose anorexia, present since she was 12, flares up during her A-Level year, leaving her in hospital. Do we need to choose between removing the incentive from Stacie or removing the opportunities from Robin and Chloe? Our sceptical interlocutor might argue that, since Stacie succeeded against the odds, others could too – if they tried hard enough.

But we see no reason to play meritocracy out to this rather brutal conclusion. This would be to concede to those who press

Stacie's case that the only benefit of primary and secondary education, the only good that would make Stacie's hard work worth it, is the qualification with which you leave. As if our schooling is a 14-year IQ test, always aiming towards the handful of letters that categorise you by your performance in GCSE and A-Level coursework and exams. But if our proposal is on the right track at all, it is because the benefits of engaging seriously in education extend far beyond the qualifications it obtains for us and the employment they make possible for us.

It's also to concede something more, and, we think, something more insidious. In all of these discussions, whether they concern benefits and welfare, the universal basic income, or admission into higher education, the language of desert is only ever used to judge those at the lower end of the social scale, those from low-income families, those from poor neighbourhoods, those who grew up in care or abusive homes. We hear talk of the deserving poor and the undeserving poor, but never of the deserving rich and the undeserving rich. Those who speak this way set the test of succeeding in spite of hardship only for those who have faced hardship. For those who haven't, including those who have experienced only privilege, we set no tests on the strength of their will power, their resolve, their tenacity and staying power. Whether you face hardship or not is, of course, a matter of luck. A central theme of this book is that we seek a system that, so far as possible, removes the influence of luck on a person's chance to explore higher education. In such a system, there is no place for the distinction between Robin and Chloe, on the one hand, and Stacie, on the other.

7

Where do the questions come from?

One of the tasks on a course like the Foundation Year in Arts and Humanities at Bristol, which is designed to lead on to a range of degree programmes, is to introduce students to the degree subjects that they might study next. The options are varied: in the first four years that the programme ran (from 2013 to 2017), students went on to 16 different degrees in the Faculty of Arts, from anthropology to theology, and five elsewhere in the university, including childhood studies, geography and law. In a seminar with the first cohort, we introduced the different degrees, including by suggesting the kinds of question that you might ask in each one. For instance, in literary study, you might ask: 'Why is this text still read after five hundred years, but not that one?' Or you might ask: '*Is* the text we are reading now the same one that was read when it was first published?'

Delia is a student who never rushes a thought. After we had given a similar introduction to other disciplines – including philosophy and history – she began to speak. "I see all of this," she said. "I hear what you're saying. But – and maybe this is just me – I don't understand: where do the questions come from?"

When we first started to think about the foundation year, in early 2012, we imagined that, at the heart of the programme would sit a 'great books' course. Around this, we would build skills training and independent study options, but the main academic content would be a sort of intellectual Grand Tour – a journey through the works of literature, history and philosophy that compose what is often referred to as the Western canon. Start with Homer's *Odyssey*, Virgil's *Aeneid*; leap forward to Dante's *Divine comedy*, Shakespeare's tragedies, Descartes' *Meditations*; forward again to the Enlightenment writings of Hume, Rousseau, Kant; and so on. One of the advantages of this approach, we thought, would be providing students with an overall narrative into which they could stitch their later studies in a particular discipline. We also hoped such an approach would make the course genuinely interdisciplinary; indeed, that it might illuminate how artificial some of the distinctions are between, say, theology and philosophy or poetry. We were excited about the opportunity to create a new curriculum of this kind, and particularly one that stretched over a long time period, and that ranged widely, asking large questions across disciplines.

This vision of the programme didn't survive long, although much of the ambition to cross time periods and disciplines remained. The 'great books' approach, it quickly became apparent, would end up being very White, very male, very European, with the leisured classes very much in evidence; and very much the 'great man' view of intellectual endeavour – the locus of cultural activity and production situated in single individuals, always men, often perceived as renegades. Our shift away from this approach happened for a variety of reasons, but a crucial one was that the endeavour of designing the course was anchored in a very particular sense of who the students might be. The fictional pen portraits, of which we gave examples in Chapter 3, were still with us, and it became apparent that we would have to test the curriculum we were designing against the experiences of those students. Freire writes:

> One cannot expect positive results from an educational or political action program which fails to respect the

particular view of the world held by the people. Such a program constitutes cultural invasion, good intentions notwithstanding. (1993, p 95)

The process of designing the curriculum involved dialogue, in a Freirian sense, initially with fictional interlocutors and later with the community partners with whom we were to develop taster courses. It also involved us acknowledging our own power, and seeking to understand how this programme needed to be established in spite of our own good intentions, rather than on the back of them. The more we tried to understand the potential worldview of the students we were seeking to recruit, the more challenges there were to the curriculum we were trying to create.

The module that was to carry the academic content in our programme was called 'What Does It Mean To Be Human?'. One of the reasons this question worked well – and a very high number of students from the first cohort said it attracted them to the programme – is that it is genuinely open-ended. Students felt they could bring their own experience and questions to the question. Given this, how could we hope to explore that question in the classroom if we drew the readings from the output of a very small, geographically parochial, homogeneous subset of humanity – White men with the influence to make their voice heard and the prestige to have it preserved? What's more, how could we claim to showcase the 'great books' that human culture has produced while limiting our attention to the works that historical accident and tradition had bequeathed to us as the best, whatever scale of goodness that's measured on? One change that we made, fairly late in the process, was to begin the module in the present day (it usually starts with a lecture on Hollywood film) and end it in antiquity, rather than the other way around. This has added to the sense of starting with present-day assumptions and probing their origins, but has also allowed us to carry contemporary questions – say, for example about women's rights – back from a contemporary lecture on the nature of work into historical sources from thousands of years ago.

Yet there continued also to be dialogue with established university structures and formal requirements for the creation of a programme: in this instance, the submission of lengthy paperwork outlining the overall structure of the programme and mapping the individual aims, outcomes, assessment and teaching modes of each module. This testing of the model against an established educational environment was important too. We thought that some of the structure of a formal education environment would be vital for those of our students who had experienced relatively chaotic lives, and that has been borne out by experience. In an earlier chapter, we heard Max Kenner talk about the Bard Prison Initiative being conservative in its pedagogy and radical in who it includes. David Watson (2009), as noted in Chapter 2, has argued that universities are *always* required to be both conservative and radical. It may be that some of the most exciting work they do is in the relationship between these two parts of their identity: sifting and conserving the treasures and ideas of the past and testing them against new perspectives and experiences.

A particular challenge for us, in creating the curriculum, was how to decolonise it. Bristol's Faculty of Arts was, at that time, dominated by White scholars and subject matter. There have been welcome changes subsequently, but as Chapter 3 demonstrated, there are major challenges to integrating Black and minority ethnic students into a structure that was originally designed to exclude them. One reason that the question that animates this book seems to us so important – the question of who universities are for (as well as against) – is that to answer it as we have done also changes radically the nature of the *intellectual* questions we ask, not just the bureaucratic ones associated with, say, admissions or, in the staff sphere, hiring and recruitment. bell hooks has written:

As a classroom community, our capacity to generate excitement is deeply affected by our interest in one another, in hearing one another's voices, in recognizing one another's presence. (hooks, 1994, p 8)

This recognition must begin in ensuring *presence*, in a range of individuals and communities being present in the classroom. But it also involves more radical acts of hearing, embedded in the kinds of question about language we explored in Chapter 3.

hooks (1994) locates the very particular power of the academy in the classroom, rather than in research. She writes:

The academy is not paradise. But learning is a place where paradise can be created. The classroom with all its limitations remains a location of possibility. In that field of possibility we have the opportunity to labour for freedom, to demand of ourselves and our comrades, an openness of mind and heart that allows us to face reality even as we collectively imagine ways to move beyond boundaries, to transgress. This is education as the practice of freedom. (p 207)

hooks also writes that: 'The classroom remains the most radical space of possibility in the academy' (1994, p 12). Her emphasis on the classroom is significant because it reminds us that *who* the university is – who is in the classroom – *is* pedagogy, and that it also represents the limits of what the university knows as a community of enquiry.

Beyond the arts and humanities

Of course, some will protest that, while such efforts to decolonise curricula are laudable in the arts and humanities, it is a sad but undeniable fact of history that most discoveries in, say, mathematics that might be suitable to teach to undergraduates were made from the 16th to the early 20th century, when the people with the time and education and social capital required to make such advances were men, were White European, and were from the middle and upper classes. While there are now many, many mathematicians from beyond those groups, they typically emerged in the mid- to late 20th century, by which time the subject was in its mature stage, so that their seminal results would be suitable material for an advanced unit, such as a Master's course or preparation for PhD study, but not Algebra 101 or Introduction to Probability. But not only this, these protesters will say. In arts and humanities subjects, to a first approximation, we study the human condition, human character and nature, and human experience. A curriculum that remains colonised and parochial excludes *voices*, of course; but it also thereby excludes *ideas* and *perspectives* on the topics it studies. This is the insight of standpoint epistemology – many insights are only available from certain standpoints, and those who lack that standpoint can only learn them from the testimony of those who have them. However, this is not true in mathematics. When you decide what to cover in the first-year statistics unit, you look to the ideas first; the person who originated them has little relevance. Or so say these protesters.

There is some truth here. But it is also worth thinking through what we are trying to do when we teach students a body of material. In some subjects – parts of engineering, dentistry, psychology, law and medicine – we teach the material in order to imprint it in the minds of our students. Their degree aims at a particular vocation and, to pursue it, students must know certain facts, acquire certain skills, and understand certain mechanisms. In these degrees, the ideas we teach are dictated by the needs of the student later in life, as well as of those with whom they will interact. There has been increasing attention in the field of medicine, for example, on the need for students to understand the 'medical humanities' or the role of creativity, or to think critically about society. After all, in most of these disciplines the student will end up interacting with – and shaping – the public and the public realm, in a variety of ways.

Not so for all degrees, though. It is a rare physics graduate who will use the 10 field equations at the heart of Einstein's theory of general relativity outside of their degree, and a rare historian who will be called on to enumerate the causes of the French Revolution in later life (although online subcultures have created unexpected uses for some forms of expertise.) So, when we design our curricula for these subjects, we have more flexibility in what we choose to teach. If one area of our subject has better gender balance, for instance, if there is some topic whose main contributors are rather less homogeneous than another, we might favour that.

Why? Well, while part of our purpose as teachers is to introduce students to new ideas, another part is to ensure that we put them in the best possible position to explore those ideas; and yet another is to ensure that they feel they could pursue the subject further should they wish to – perhaps so far that they start to contribute novel ideas and insights to it themselves. But is it more difficult to pursue a subject further when you hear no voices and see no faces like yours among the assigned reading? What conclusion might you draw about the way in which your future contributions will be valued? In Chapter 3, we saw an example of this in practice, in which Nina responded to a voice she recognised – that of Gayatri Chakravorty Spivak – but in which she also recognised the process through which that voice was being marginalised in the academy (by being dismissed as 'difficult'). This is a reminder that part of what we teach students is also implicit, rather than just explicit and content-driven: we teach them that *these* voices are valued, and *those* are not. One of the points that Nina's story makes clear is the pressure that is consequently placed on an individual, who finds nobody 'like them' on the sanctioned list of the good and the great of the discipline. What stores of self-confidence would you have to draw on, what sense of self-worth would you already need to have, in order to overcome the inevitable doubts about your ability that come with any sort of study?

Another possibility: at least in universities in the UK, science, engineering and medical departments spend little time teaching their students the history or philosophy of the topics they cover. Much of the material is taught ahistorically, the ideas presented in their finished, polished form, with little more than a glance at the story behind their discovery or invention. This often means losing the opportunity to understand the nature of scientific progress – the trials and errors that lead towards it, the gradually dawning understanding that accompanies it. But it also prevents us from understanding the historical context of the ideas. Why was the discovery made then? Why did that person, from that social group, make the discovery, rather than someone else? Why is that person's name associated with the invention, while others contributed just as many ideas? What were the political consequences of this discovery? Were political motivations behind the research that led to it? If we were to teach these questions in more depth, we could go some way to decolonising our science curricula by exploring together with students the racism, the sexism, the social hierarchies, the barriers and the prejudices that led to the exclusion of certain individuals from participating in the science of their day.[19]

There are two further objections to this position that are worth considering. One is the question of whether this analysis ignores the role of empathy. Why is it that, for example, a student would identify more with a thinker who shares their gender, ethnicity, first language, or even just the same century? What about historical and cross-cultural empathy by which, for example, a young woman in her thirties might identify with the younger hero of a Victorian novel, for reasons that might be difficult to ascribe? A related question here is about 'quality'. A novel of that kind – *David Copperfield* by Charles Dickens, say, or George Eliot's *Daniel Deronda* – has proved culturally resilient, has been tested and retested against the taste of many readers in different places and times. Is there a risk that it falls out of the canon and is replaced with a novel that meets currently fashionable concerns, but which has less capacity to be reread and rethought by countless readers in future?

It may be helpful to think about these questions by returning to David Watson's insight that universities are intrinsically both conservative *and* radical. Some of the difficulties in this debate are when we see the institution as becoming one or other of these entirely: rejecting *Jane Eyre* in favour of *Wide Sargasso Sea*, for example, or rejecting the latter by an insistence on the superiority of the former. In either case, there is a risk that we cease to be curious. So, one argument might be that we want to read *both* of these texts. Another might be to acknowledge the creativity involved in rereading and rewriting. One of the powers in *Wide Sargasso Sea* is that it tells the story of *Jane Eyre* again, from a different standpoint. In doing so, it also provides a model for how we as readers might integrate – and create – new readings of older texts (see Willis, 2017).

Penny Jane Burke (2012) notes that 'it is important to strongly emphasize' that the sort of changes she advocates to higher education are 'not about lowering of standards or creating subs-standard courses and degrees. Indeed [this] is about strengthening standards and quality, as it requires all participants in higher education to develop deeper levels of criticality and reflexivity' (p 195). Burke quotes Freire:

> There is no genuine instruction in whose process no research is performed by way of question, investigation, curiosity, creativity just as there is no research in the course of which researchers do not learn – after all, by coming to know, they learn, and after having learned something, they communicate, they teach. The role of the university... is to immerse itself, utterly seriously, in the moment of this circle. (Cited in Burke, p 196)

One advantage of the model of universities we propose, if fully realised, is that academics themselves would continue to learn much more explicitly, by taking modules outside their own disciplines – in which they would be beginners alongside others at very different stages of their overall education. Perhaps nothing produces equality in the classroom so much as an expert in one field becoming a beginner again, and a classroom in which people with radically different social positions interact on equal terms exemplifies the possibilities of democracy. A desire to create the 'moment of this circle' also motivates the proposals outlined here for a course in which students are tasked with sharing what they learn in some form, and thus also that they might 'having learned something' also go on to 'communicate' and 'teach' it.

Local histories

After abandoning our plans for an ancient-to-modern tour through the official European canon, we turned next to a local-to-global tour through the broader world of ideas instead. Start with issues local in both time and place – issues that arise in modern-day Bristol and for the sorts of people we hoped to attract to our programme – and travel outwards, away from Bristol and backwards in time. Our intention was to make the programme more accessible; to make the material more relevant, less daunting, more engaging. But those who come to higher education later in their lives – like many who come to it earlier but from situations with sparse intellectual opportunities – sometimes know more than enough about their local situations; indeed, they are quite often fed up with a certain sort of cultural or intellectual parochialism that has characterised their lives thus far. They may also wish to choose for themselves how they integrate what they know from 'outside' the academy, rather than seeing it re-presented on someone else's terms. Indeed, there is a risk of repeating an experience that working-class communities, for example, often report: that they are often denied the opportunities to be narrators of their own experience. Meanwhile, some individuals seek higher education precisely so that they might break out from the situation they have inhabited, with workmates, perhaps, who have no interest in academic pursuits, or parents or friends who actively decry them. Those who identify as a minority gender – trans men and women, genderqueer and non-binary people – often praise the internet for connecting them to others who identify in the same way and thereby allowing them to have conversations that they couldn't have before. Higher education can do this too – it can connect students with ideas they haven't encountered before and put them into dialogue with those ideas in a way that is important to them. It can break them out of the circle of ideas and interlocutors with which they have interacted so far.

So the danger in designing a programme that will attract people because of its direct relevance to their lives is that this accepts the modern assumption that education must fit a narrow definition of practical use, and it adds to the patronising assumption that this is particularly true for those traditionally excluded from higher education. Max Kenner, founder of the Bard Prison Initiative (BPI), notes that "what is liberating for our students" at the BPI is "that they are considered students". Yet he notes that policy discussions about prison education overwhelmingly revert to "mak[ing] these projects about the prison…. You do that and you're dead." Thus it is framed as if exploring the broad array of human knowledge may be a luxury afforded to the middle classes and the wealthy who compose the current student body, but to attract others, it must be made more relevant to their daily concerns. Kenner notes with frustration: "It's almost as if the more successful our students are in the prisons the more people just start to see us as some kind of unicorn, as some kind of magical aberration that has less to do with anything else." Yet just as traditional university students often crave an education that really broadens their field of view, indeed, allows them to escape what they have experienced so far in their lives, it has been our experience that a broader range of adults who have experienced complex lives want this too.

Often, but not always. There are also those who come to university hoping to understand something of direct relevance to their lives. And herein lies the difficulty in designing a curriculum for this new conception of the university. How do you marry the directly relevant, the applicable, and the immediately useful to that which lies beyond what might ever guide the student in their lives, the material that might connect the student with a whole new set of ideas? We'll sketch some possibilities here. But we must emphasise that the possibility of a university of this kind does not stand or fall with the viability of these courses. For many who wish to see a more accessible, inclusive, fairer university system, the only issue is access. What we teach in our universities at present should remain largely intact, such people will say, perhaps with some shift towards a more inclusive and representative curriculum. We might call this *a liberal approach* – it leaves intact what is taught in the classroom, but tries to change who is in the classroom where it is taught. And, while we don't agree with it, the name is not intended to be pejorative. But for others, and we include ourselves in this, access is not the only problem: what is taught in the classroom often itself excludes; the very questions we ask must change, just as those permitted to contribute to answering them must also change, for those questions may well contain assumptions that hold only from the parochial view discussed above. For instance, when liberal feminists like Betty Friedan asked how we could get more women into the workforce, radical feminists like bell hooks countered that there were plenty there already, in low-paid, stultifying, undervalued jobs, and we should be asking instead how we might make the workplace more bearable for those women. hooks (2003) makes a comparable point about the diversity of universities:

Time and time again I have observed white peers working to unlearn white supremacy as they become aware of the reality that they have little contact with non-white people. They open their 'eyes' and see that there were always non-white folks around them that they did not 'see' when they were blinded by white privilege stemming from racist foundations. Time and time again I come to do anti-racist work at liberal arts colleges that I am told are 'all white' only to find that the majority of support staff and service workers are non-white. (pp 36-7)

A truly radical university would rethink its membership so that the boundaries between being a staff member and student, or between support staff and academics, becomes increasingly porous.

Towards a new curriculum

A truly radical curriculum for universities would see students set the questions themselves, perhaps in collaboration with their lecturers, and their courses would seek to answer them. We have taken this route for two of the courses we have devised, but not for the other two. Why not? Well, setting questions is itself a skill, and learning it is every bit as much a part of education as learning the questions that others have asked and the answers they've given, and how to come by your own answers to those questions. Freire himself – a proponent of radically decentring classrooms – came, over the course of his career, to believe the expertise of the teacher still had a place in the dialogue he advocated (see Beckett, 2013). With that in mind, then, we propose our own questions for two of the courses suggested, though more advanced modules might deviate from this structure. Indeed, rather than traditional courses, which often grow out of a motley of questions directed towards a single theme or author or historical event but all approached from the vantage point of a single discipline, we propose modules based on single questions but drawing on a wide range of disciplines to explore the possible answers.

Here are three questions for students:

- Humans, non-human animals, and even plants learn about the world around them, albeit incompletely and often inaccurately. How would you build a robot capable of learning about the world around it?
- A democracy is a system of government in which certain decisions – fiscal, legislative, and so on – are delegated to a small group, who members are elected by some system of voting with a wide suffrage. What is the best democratic system? Does it depend on what the country is like? If so, in what ways?
- How might what you are learning on your programme of study be shared with others?

And here is a question for the communities around the university:

- What are the most important, urgent, useful, or interesting questions we should ask in the classroom this year?

To answer either of the first two questions, we must call on the resources of a number of different disciplines. From the literary scholars and the historians, we might learn how robots have been viewed in the past. As our colleague Genevieve Liveley from the Classics department explained to the foundation students in her lecture on androids, we find talk of human–machine hybrids as far back as Homer in antiquity, and they have played an important role in much speculative fiction since (see also Liveley, 2006). And literature has long been a source of inspiration for technological innovation, providing a testing ground in our collective imaginations for future developments.

From philosophers, we might learn about the goals at which our robot should aim. Should it simply aim to stockpile as many facts as possible, or do we want it to be able to fit these facts together in the manner characteristic of understanding? Do we want it simply to learn what has happened so far in the world, or do we want it to be able to predict the future with some accuracy? So the philosopher, as is her wont, compels us to make the meaning of our question more precise; to make our goal clearer. From the psychologists, we might learn the ways in which humans and non-human animals learn about the world – that is, we learn how evolution has addressed the problem we have set ourselves. From the computer scientists and statisticians, we learn about statistical reasoning, data mining and machine learning. The engineers teach us about existing technology and the limitations we currently face. And the social scientists teach us the potential risks that lie in automated learning. Even now, for instance, we know how prejudiced attitudes in society are replicated by machine-learning algorithms trained on data sets that reflect those attitudes: an algorithm designed to detect criminal behaviour that is trained on the behaviour of those currently incarcerated will replicate the racist bias of the criminal justice system, which locks up people of colour more often and for longer sentences than White people accused of the same crimes.

Just as the material covered in such a module would be varied – traversing the university's departments from Classics to computer science to psychology – so would the forms of assessment used. Students might choose the traditional option of individual, essay-based coursework, either writing on a single topic covered – how were robots portrayed in the literature of antiquity? – or on some combination of them – what are the ethical concerns with current machine learning and its use in the public sphere, and how might we address this? Or they might produce a creative response, such as the ones presented in Classical or recent literature, imagining the future role of technology in words, music, visual art or in various forms of making – textiles, pottery, machinery or in digital form. Or they might choose group work, producing a collaborative piece of work addressing some feasible portion of the question that defines the unit, and requires them to draw on many of the different disciplines that contribute to the unit.

A module based on the second question might have a similar structure. It might draw on work in psychology about how people make political decisions and the ways in which they can be manipulated, and on work in politics detailing the various existing voting systems around the world; from historians, we might learn how democracy emerged around the world and the ways in which it is and has been threatened, whether from voter suppression, district gerrymandering, or from polarisation of public opinion; and philosophers might train us in how to think about how widely we should cast the suffrage – from what age? Citizens, residents, both? The possibility that you might forfeit your vote by breaking the law?

And, again, we might use a variety of forms of assessment: essays, exam, group projects, group presentations. In this case, perhaps the group project might be undertaken with a partner organisation outside higher education. Perhaps there is a local group of activists with whom students might collaborate on a joint project on how to advocate for better democratic institutions. Or there might be a local community organisation that is interested in designing a democratic structure for its own decision making – how it picks a chairperson, for instance, or how it decides to spend its money. Or it could be a lobby group – a disability action group, for instance – that wants to ensure that it is representing the views of everyone on whose behalf it lobbies policymakers.

The third question we have set for students is different, in that it is open for the student to define both what they are learning and what is meant by it being 'shared'. At its heart, this module is designed to do two things. Stanley Cavell (2006) has written:

'At some point in teaching the pupil must go on and want to go alone' (p 114). This work is designed to help the student 'go on' with the material they have been studying, without their teacher (if not alone). The second goal of this module is to lead the student to think of knowledge as inherently social; to consider the various ways in which it might be shared, the potential benefits of doing so, as well as the risks: and the modes in which knowledge can be used to dominate, silence and repress. It is thus also designed to help them to become themselves a 'representative' of the discipline and, potentially, of the university (if not an uncritical one), in a way that might shift their relationships to being 'inside' the academy. This would not mean simply reproducing an institutional approach, but would mean 'becoming' part of the discipline and the university in ways that we usually associate with a later stage in student or career development. This potentially has radical implications for who 'is' the university and at what stage in their engagement with it.

As we imagine it, a question of this kind would ideally be pursued across a student's programme of study, rather than in a single course. In the part-time BA in English Literature and Community Engagement (ELCE), for example, students take one 20-credit module of this kind in each of the first four years of their six-year course. Building on the ELCE structure, in the course we imagine, students' engagement with the question might progress through a variety of stages. In the first stage, the student would encounter theoretical perspectives on how knowledge is 'shared', including ideas from postcolonial theory, as well as fields such as organisational studies, to provide an understanding of how institutions manage and disseminate information. In this stage, students would also reflect on what they are learning, and the assessment might be in the form of a learning auto/ethnography, in which the students present a case study of their own learning story, or of someone else they have interviewed, and the institutions, individuals and assumptions that have shaped it.

In the second stage, the student would consider the various modes in which they might 'share' what they are learning. Sometimes this would be a direct and explicit relationship: so, a history student might run events with a local history society, or engage with an existing school project on the First World War. For other students, it would be implicit: a student might be reading about ecocriticism in film and might volunteer in an industry promoting renewable energy. In the third stage, the student would reflect on the impact of the work they are doing, by interviewing participants, through external or peer review or by gathering statistical data (as appropriate). In the fourth stage, the student would consider whether the work they are doing is sustainable, and in what form, or what kind of end it reaches.

The fourth question we propose is deliberately open and would be designed to run alongside a participatory budgeting model. Our experience, in building taster courses, is that new questions emerge by involving a different range of participants in curriculum design. In Chapter 3, Mwenza Blell describes a course in which this process unfolded within the course itself, as each week students were asked what they wanted to learn the following week. Our hope would be to make the process of posing questions not one that belongs solely with the 'experts' (although they have a role), but one in which community participants would regularly and formally play a part. These questions would thus arise out of experience. This would allow universities to be places that would be much more responsive to change, whether the changes individuals are experiencing in their lives (family breakdown, illness, bereavement, changes of place, loss of income and so on) or those that society faces, such as climate change or changes in health outcomes and inequalities. It would also enable a greater understanding of the 'causes' and 'effects' of these changes, and of the way in which these categories are permeable: a family breakdown might be felt as the cause of an individual's worsened mental health, but could also be understood as in itself an effect of wider economic change in society. Perhaps most significantly, it would ensure all of us recognise – as Delia did – that the starting point for any field of enquiry is itself built on assumptions, which we do not always see. A much broader range of individuals would thus be involved in asking new questions and in reconfiguring old ones in unexpected ways.

CONCLUSION

The university-without-walls

We're in the basement of a café. It's set up for a comedy show or perhaps an open mic night. But now, 25 people are gathered to talk about collective action. A representative from the local branch of the Fire Brigades Union starts the event off. He tells the history of strikes his union has been involved in, from the unqualified success of 1977 to the partial victories of 2002 and 2015. He talks about the difficulty of retaining public support, particularly if the media becomes hostile; how to tell when the employers are prepared to make a deal; knowing where the levers of power are. Next up, it's two professors from the university's Law School, experts in labour law and company law. They wrote an article on the legal side of industrial action 10 years ago, and they walk the audience through it. And, finally, a student – he draws on the strike tactics used in labour movements around the world, highlighting what we might learn from them. The discussion proceeds at pace – each speaker contributes the knowledge they've brought with them, historical, political, or legal, and the other discussants raise questions, make suggestions, explain how a particular proposal might play out for them, identify where there are gaps in our collective knowledge and further work needed. The session is 'horizontal' or 'decentred'.

One of the student organisers is chairing, and does it well, but otherwise everyone is there as an equal.

As we drew near to completing this book, large numbers of lecturers, professors, teaching fellows, research managers, student support staff, finance administrators and library staff from universities around the UK came out on strike to protest about changes to their pension scheme – changes that had been pursued by the senior management of universities without consultation and in defiance of the evidence. Over the 14 days of the strike, the university burst out of its buildings and reassembled in twos and threes and larger groups on the picket lines outside the usual teaching spaces, in rallies outside the offices of the senior management, on marches through the centre of town, and in impromptu 'teach outs' organised in small venues around the city, such as the café described above. It was a brief glimpse of what Adrienne Rich called the 'university-without-walls'. As a result of undemocratic leadership by those running universities, those who carry out its central work created democratic forms of learning outside its walls.

The mood on the picket line was varied, of course, but it was often creative. One of our colleagues turned up on International Women's Day, which was during the strike, with a beautiful piece of embroidery in suffragette colours, reading 'A woman's place is in the resistance.' I took a picture of her holding it, and she said: "As soon as we are back at work that's going up in my office." The trust that was created by the strike allowed many staff to be more open, more silly, more personal – and more vulnerable – with one another. In part, this seemed to be to do with stepping away from their particular fields of expertise and into a shared field of experience. We were all going through something together. And we began to talk much more about things other than work: house moves, pets, families, films, even our own childhoods. In a long conversation with one colleague, I discovered that we had both been home schooled by 'back-to-the-land' parents. Without the strike, we might never have discovered that (and I doubt that either of us would have guessed). We allowed our life experiences to come into our work relationships much more than we normally would. I can only speak for myself, of course, but for me it brought a real feeling of authenticity and closeness.

The strike also seemed to give a sense of common purpose to people working across a wide range of disciplines, and in many different roles in the university. For years there has been rhetoric within UK universities telling us to 'de-silo' and yet it seemed to take a strike to make it happen. It was exhilarating to realise that in fact we all share a sense of what the university should be for, as well as a common set of frustrations. The strike also put people centre stage who normally don't get much of a voice in a university: academic-related staff, postgraduates, hourly paid teachers, people on short-term contracts, Black and Asian minority ethnic staff, people at the beginning of their careers. Often those with the most to lose were the boldest in speaking out and showing leadership. This could be sobering: some colleagues reported leaving rallies feeling uplifted, while others felt drained or vulnerable.

It may sound idealistic to think that any of this energy could be repurposed for the day-to-day business of university organisation. But why not? The one experience that the three authors of this book have shared that was similar was the creation of the foundation year, which is discussed in these pages. It too involved doing something new – going into uncharted territory. In conventional academic departments, we are always building on an existing curriculum and way of doing things. That gives great stability, but it also means change is inevitably incremental (and often resisted). There's something liberating about feeling that you are creating rather than revising, and universities need to be doing both. That programme also involved stepping outside of usual silos; in this case, by teaching in unconventional ways across disciplines. And it created some of the same risks, including that the responsibility for change was borne disproportionately by those with most to lose: staff in vulnerable positions (in the case of the strike) and adults from a variety of complex backgrounds who took a chance on returning to education (on the foundation year).

Rebecca Solnit (2010) writes:

> Few speak of paradise now, except as something remote enough to be impossible. The ideal societies we hear of are mostly far away or long ago or both…. The implication is that we here and now are far from capable of living such ideals. But what if paradise flashed up among us from time to time – at the worst of times? What if we glimpsed it in the jaws of hell? These flashes may give us, as the long ago and far away do not, a glimpse of who else we ourselves may be and what else our society could become. (p 9)

Solnit's interest is in disasters such as the San Francisco earthquake in 1906 or the impact of Hurricane Katrina on New Orleans in 2005. In the examples she traces, she finds evidence of people living generously and finding alternative ways of organising society, at a moment when the conventional structures have broken down.

The strike was not a comparable 'disaster', but it was a moment when the existing structures failed and were made visible, and alternative forms of organisation briefly sprang up in their place. Solnit's vision has particular urgency given the devastating social, economic and environmental changes that may engulf human society in the next hundred years. Universities will need new ways of organising themselves – to work across disciplines, and with the whole of society – if they are to help us find alternative ways of living and of understanding radically different circumstances.

The academy is not paradise, as bell hooks reminds us, although it is sometimes possible to be seduced by nostalgia for an earlier era (far away and long ago), as we discussed in the Introduction.

But the academy remains a place, as hooks writes too, 'where paradise can be created'. This book suggests some alternative ways of organising universities, in the meantime. The changes that we propose would allow lifelong access to higher education. They would change the way that universities are funded, moving from individually accrued debt to a modest participation tax. They would – we hope – make higher education accessible to a much wider range of people, and would break down some of the socioeconomic and cultural barriers to access. Doing all of this would, we argue, have a profound impact on the nature of the university itself, allowing a much more productive exchange between expertise and experience than is currently possible. It would change not only who universities are for, but also what they are for.

Like the strike, and like working on the foundation year, this book has in its own way felt risky and unlike the writing that each of us has done separately. It arises from shared experiences that the three of us have had, but also out of debates and discussions between us and with our colleagues, students and friends outside the academy. We hope that the book is an unfinished conversation and that it leaves space for the reader to reimagine who may be the university in the future and, as a consequence, what else our universities could become.

Appendix: Written work for application to the Foundation Year in Arts and Humanities (2017)

Please write an essay of between 1,000 and 1,500 words, following the instructions given below. The work should be emailed to xxx@bristol.ac.uk no later than Friday 10th March. Please be sure to state your name on the essay.

If you have any questions about how to approach this essay, please e-mail Richard Pettigrew at yyy@bris.ac.uk.

The essay should address the question 'What does it mean to be human?' and should compare and contrast **two** of the works from the list below.

Choose **two** of the five options:

- a poem called 'Two lorries' by Seamus Heaney;
- a painting called 'Five' by Lubaina Himid;
- an extract from *Representation* by Stuart Hall;
- an extract from *What does it all mean?* by Thomas Nagel;
- a film of your choice, or a particular scene from a film.

Please note that no wider/further research or reading is expected or required in completing this essay. We are looking for responses that engage with two of these works as they are presented here. You should respond to the question and to two of the works in your own words and in your own way.

If you are unsure how to start or how to structure your essay, you may wish to think about some or all of the following questions:

- How do the works you have chosen address the question 'What does it mean to be human?' Do they address this question directly or indirectly? What conclusions are reached about what it means to be human (or to be a 'person')? What is seen as important to, essential in, or of value for a human life in this work?
- How is each work structured? How does it start and end? What does it include or exclude? What kind of language is used (if relevant)?
- Is there anything you are particularly interested by in each work, which relates to its presentation of what human life is like or has been like in the past? Why does this particular aspect of the work interest you?
- Did you learn anything new from either or both of the works about what it means to be human?
- Were you left with any questions about either of the works? Is there anything you are not sure you understand about either of them, or that you would like to know more about?
- How does the form of each of these works shape the content? In other words: How is the question 'What does it mean to be human?' addressed differently in a poem, or a philosophical essay, or a painting, or a film? How might the content of the poem be different if it were presented in a photograph? Might the Nagel extract be rewritten as a poem? In each case, would the question be addressed *differently*, if the form of the work changed?

Notes

[1] For a discussion of the term 'working class' and the 'complexity around the many different ways of embodying working-classness', see Reay (2017), pp 1-10. We follow Reay in seeing the term 'working class' as of ongoing significance, including in understanding the relationships that a range of individuals and communities have with education.

[2] This would build on existing good practice. For example, in 1987, after serious industrial disputes, the car manufacturer Ford put aside 0.3% of its annual wage bill for an Employee Development and Assistance Programme (EDAP). Members of staff could apply for up to £200 per year for learning that was not related to the business, whether it was an exercise class or a university course. The EDAP scheme's benefits have been wide-ranging: improved staff retention, reduced absenteeism, better industrial relations, and knock-on effects on work-based learning and on family learning schemes. Universities would be ideally placed to help stimulate a much larger learning culture of this kind, working with other sectors and providers (Tuckett 1991, pp 17-18).

[3] This is based on the following assumptions:

- UK population is 70 million;
- 80% of population is aged 18 or over – that is, 56 million;
- 90% of adults aged 18 or over participate – that is, 50 million;
- on average, those who participate take 80 free credits over the course of 60 years of their life (age 18-78) (and thus 1.333 credits per year);
- it costs £1,500 to teach a 20-credit point module on average (and thus £75 per credit point on average).

The calculation then runs as follows:
70,000,000 x 0.8 x 0.9 x 1.333 x £75 = £5,038,740,000

[4] Our calculation is based on the same assumptions used by Green and Mason, but with our amended figures, and assuming that nearly all eligible existing graduates accumulate 240 credits or more, and including those over 64 years old in the taxation. The latter increases the pool of those eligible for taxation from 4.6 million to 6 million, but the percentage in the higher rate of tax is lower, as is the mean income for this group.

[5] The revenue from the graduate tax is as follows:

(70million*0.9*0.8*0.3*(£26,000-£11,000)*0.05) +
  (70million*0.9*0.8*0.6*(£26,000-£11,000)*0.015) +
    (70million*0.9*0.8*0.3*(£48,000-£45,000)*0.15*0.01) +
      (70million*0.9*0.8*0.6*(£48,000-£45,000)*0.15*0.02)

$\approx$ £18.5billion

The cost of higher education under the assumptions mentioned is:

(0.4*70million*0.9*0.8*(180*£75)/60)) +
  (0.6*70million*0.9*0.8*(360*£75)/60))

$\approx$ £18.1billion

[6] See http://nmite.org.uk/about.

[7] All quotations from Nina are from an interview with the author on 1 April 2016.

[8] We are grateful to the researcher, Fran Johnson, for permission to reproduce this material and the longer quotation from an interview with Simon that follows. For a more detailed account of this research, see Johnson (forthcoming).

[9] All quotations from Mwenza Blell are from an interview with the author on 31 December 2017.

[10] All quotations from Max Kenner are from an interview with the author on 21 December 2017.

[11] For a wider perspective on the BPI, see Lagemann (2017). For other connections between prisons and universities in the US, it is worth looking at the Prison University Project at San Quentin State Prison, Jennifer Lackey's courses at Stateville Correctional Center in Illinois, and Columbia's Justice-in-Education Initiative.

[12] This from a study of admissions to our own institution (Hoare and Johnston, 2010, pp 37-38):

> Among the cohorts of students admitted to the University of Bristol, those who attended independent schools performed better in the A-level examinations than those who attended

state schools. But they did not also outperform students from state schools in their university degree programmes: indeed, they were less likely to get a first-class degree and more likely to get a lower second-class grade or less. This difference holds even when A-level performance is taken into account: students with high A-level scores are more likely to get first-class degrees, for example, but students from state schools with such high scores are more likely to achieve the highest degree grade than are students with similar scores who attended independent schools.

This from a study of medical school admissions in the UK (Kumwenda et al, 2017):

Students from independent schools had significantly higher mean UKCAT (UK Clinical Aptitude Test) scores than students from state-funded schools. Similarly, students from independent schools came into medical school with significantly higher mean GAMSAT (Graduate Medical School Admissions Test) scores than students from state-funded schools. However, students from state-funded schools were almost twice as likely to finish in the highest rank of the EPM ranking than those who attended independent schools.

[13] See www.cao.cam.ac.uk/behind-the-headlines/importance-of-aslevel; www.cao.cam.ac.uk/admissions-research/alevel-predictor; www.cao.cam.ac.uk/admissions-research/alevels-degree-potential. See also Johnston et al (2015).

[14] From a report by HEFCE (2014a): '72% of White students who entered higher education with BBB gained a first or upper second. This compares with 56% for Asian students, and 53% for Black students, entering with the same A-level grades.'

[15] The French system differs from our proposal in some important respects: there, the learner contribution (or tuition fees) starts immediately, though it is only a fraction of the current level in the UK; in France, applicants must have passed their high school exams (the *Baccalaureate*), while the UK does not even require passes at A-Level or equivalent; the UK system offers 60 credits before an admission point, whereas the French system offers a full

year – essentially, the admission to the second year of a degree programme is based on achievement in the first year, as is the case currently in the UK for students who enter through our selective admissions procedure. Note also that the French higher education system includes not only the *université* component, but also the *grandes écoles* component, which has no opposite number in the UK – the *grandes écoles* are extremely prestigious institutions that train the political and economic elite of the country; admission to these institutions is highly selective and extremely competitive.

[16] Another problem is what is usually rather brutally termed 'attrition', that is, how many students will end up not completing the course of study that they originally wanted to undertake? Here the evidence pulls in opposite directions: the number of Open University students who do not complete their degree has never been as high as sceptics feared when it was initiated, but it is nonetheless higher than for other universities – and harder to measure, since students enrol with a range of aims including in relation to how long a course of study they may undertake (see Ashby, 2004). The French system is changing to a selective system closer to our current model in the UK precisely because so-called dropout rates were very high on the non-selective model – around three in every five students dropped out or failed before the start of the second year of their degree. It is clear that, within the system we propose, ongoing advice and guidance would be vital – both to direct potential students to the modules they might most enjoy and thrive on, but also to help students who find they have taken a wrong turn or who encounter a subject that (for whatever reason) is off-putting. Another feature that we hope will mitigate attrition rates is the possibility of trying 40 credits' worth of material that you then opt out of. This will allow students to test what interests them, what material they find manageable, and so on. And as well as having students trial modules by enrolling on them, online material for courses – lecture videos, interactive materials, reading lists, past papers, and so on – allows students to trial them before they commit even to that extent. But it is also worth emphasising that 'dropping out' would have different connotations in the system we propose. Some evidence suggests that a very high percentage of Open University students accumulate credits, but a relatively low percentage reach graduation. In a system that emphasises credit accumulation rather than the degree structure, the former group would be counted as successful students. This is not just

a statistical sleight of hand: Simon's story, and others like it, show that our current system *constructs* success and failure in very particular ways.

[17] For a similar point about the disconnect between academic experts and the rest of a community in the context of feminist theory and the relation of feminist intellectuals and academics to the rest of the feminist movement, see hooks (2000): '[a] tug-of-war … has existed within [the] feminist movement between feminist intellectuals and academics, and participants in the movement who equate education with bourgeois privilege and are fiercely anti-intellectual' (p 113).

[18] In the following blog hosted by the leading scientific journal *Nature*, the Harvard economists Richard Freeman and Wei Huang discuss their recent research on this question: www.nature.com/news/collaboration-strength-in-diversity-1.15912. The article they discuss is Freeman and Huang (2015).

[19] Thanks to Sorana Vieru for this suggestion.

References

Adams, T. (2013) 'Doreen Lawrence: "I could have shut myself away, but that's not me"', *The Guardian*, 20 April. Available at: www.theguardian.com/uk/2013/apr/20/doreen-lawrence-stephen-lawrence.

Ahmed, S. (2012) *On being included: Racism and diversity in institutional life*, Durham and London: Duke University Press.

Appadurai, A. (2000) 'Grassroots globalisation and the research imagination', *Public Culture*, 12, pp 1-19.

Arendt, H. (1971) 'Thinking and moral considerations: a lecture', *Social Research*, pp 417-46.

Ashby, A. (2004) 'Monitoring student retention in the Open University: definition, measurement, interpretation and action', *Open Learning*, 19(1), pp 65-77.

Bacevic, J. (2018) 'Is there such a thing as a centrist higher education policy?'. Available at: https://janabacevic.net/2018/01/13/is-there-such-a-thing-as-centrist-higher-education-policy/.

BBC (2014) 'WEA centre shuts doors after 100 years empowering adults', 9 June. Available at: www.bbc.co.uk/news/uk-northern-ireland-27760313.

Beard, M. (2013) 'What are universities (not) doing about "social exclusion"? Some myths…', *Times Literary Supplement*, 20 June, p 13.

Beckett, K.S. (2013) 'Paulo Freire and the concept of education', *Educational Philosophy and Theory*, 45(1), pp 49-62.

Blackman, T. (2015) 'Why British universities should rethink selecting students by academic ability', *The Conversation*, 17 August. Available at: https://theconversation.com/why-british-universities-should-rethink-selecting-students-by-academic-ability-45473.

Blair, I.V., Ma, J.E. and Lenton, A.P. (2001) 'Imagining stereotypes away: the moderation of implicit stereotypes through mental imagery', *Journal of Personality and Social Psychology*, 81(5), pp 828-41.

Boliver, V. (2013) 'How fair is access to more prestigious UK universities?', *British Journal of Sociology*, 64(2), pp 344 64.

Booth, M. (2017) '£75m new library for Bristol Uni as half of city's libraries set to close', *Bristol 24/7*, 5 Sept. Available at: www.bristol247.com/news-and-features/news/75m-new-library-bristol-uni-half-citys-libraries-close.

Bordalo, P., Coffman, K., Gennaioli, N. and Shleifer, A. (2016) 'Stereotypes', *The Quarterly Journal of Economics*, 131(4), pp 1753-94.

Bristol SU (Students' Union) (2016) 'BME Attainment Gap Report'. Available at: www.bristol.ac.uk/media-library/sites/sraa/bme-attainment-gap-report.pdf.

Burke, P.J. (2012) *The right to higher education: Beyond widening participation*, Abingdon: Routledge.

Butcher, J., Clarke, A., McPherson, E., Wood, C., Johnson, F., Sperlinger, T., Harman, K. and Fraser, L. (2017) *Understanding the impact of outreach on access to higher education for disadvantaged adult learners*, Bristol: Office for Fair Access.

Cable, V. (2010) 'Oral statement to Parliament', 3 June. Available at: www.gov.uk/government/speeches/vince-cables-keynote-speech-on-growth.

Callender, C. (2017) 'Part-time student numbers are plummeting – here's why', *Prospect Magazine*, 30 June. Available at: www.prospectmagazine.co.uk/politics/part-time-student-numbers-are-plummeting-why-higher-education-university.

Callender, C. and Mason, G. (2017) 'Does student loan debt deter higher education participation? New evidence from England', *The ANNALS of the American Academy of Political and Social Science*, 671(1), pp 20–48.

Callender, C. and Thompson, J. (2018) *The lost part-timers: The decline of part-time undergraduate higher education in England*, London: Sutton Trust.

Carel, H. (2014) 'The philosophical role of illness', *Metaphilosophy*, 45(1), pp 20–40.

Cavell, S. (2006) *Philosophy the day after tomorrow*, Boston, MA: Harvard University Press.

Chaudhary, N. (2014) 'The fight for East Palo Alto: where does Stanford lie?', *The Stanford Daily*, 2 October. Available at: www.stanforddaily.com/2014/10/02/the-fight-for-east-palo-alto-where-does-stanford-lie.

CIPD (Chartered Institute of Personnel and Development) (2015) *Over-qualification and skills mismatch in the graduate labour market*, London: CIPD.

Collini, S. (2012) *What are universities for?*, London: Penguin.

Conway, J.M., Jako, R.A. and Goodman, D.F. (1995) 'A meta-analysis of interrater and internal consistency reliability of selection interviews', *Journal of Applied Psychology*, 80(5), pp 565–79.

Coulson, S., Garforth, l., Payne, G. and Wastell, E. (2017) 'Admissions, adaptations and anxieties: social class inside and outside the elite university', in R. Waller, N. Ingram and M. Ward (eds) *Degrees of injustice: Social class inequalities in university admissions, experiences and outcomes*, Abingdon: Routledge.

Davis, P. (2003) 'The place of the implicit in literary discovery: creating new courses', in T. Agathocleous and A.C. Dean, *Teaching Literature: A Companion*, London: Palgrave. pp. 149–162.

Dearing, R. (1997) *Higher education in the learning society*, London: Her Majesty's Stationery Office.

Donnelly, M. and Gamsu, S. (2018) *Home and away: Social, ethnic and spatial inequalities in student mobility*, London: Sutton Trust.

Dorling, D. and Gietel-Basten, S. (2018), 'UK life expectancy has stopped rising – and austerity could be to blame', *Prospect Magazine*, 4 January. Available at: www.prospectmagazine.co.uk/politics/uk-life-expectancy-has-stopped-rising-and-austerity-could-be-to-blame.

Freeman, R.B. and Huang, W. (2015) 'Collaborating with people like me: ethnic coauthorship within the United States', *Journal of Labor Economics*, 33, no. S1 (Part 2): S289-S318.

Freire, P. (1993) *Pedagogy of the oppressed*, Trans. M. Bergman Ramos, London: Continuum.

Gamsu, S. (2015) 'The logic of the ladder – elite widening participation and the implicit "scholarship boy" discourses which never went away', https://solgamsu.wordpress.com/2015/06/16/the-logic-of-the-ladder-elite-widening-participation-and-the-implicit-scholarship-boy-discourse-which-never-went-away/comment-page-1.

Gifford, D. and Seidman, R.J. (2008) *Ulysses annotated: Revised and expanded edition*, Oakland, CA: University of California Press.

Green, A. and Mason, G. (2017) *The case for an all-age graduate tax in England*, London: Centre for Learning and Life Chances in Knowledge Economies and Societies.

Hardy, T. (2016) *Jude the Obscure* (3rd edn), New York, NY: Norton.

Harford, J. (2008) 'The admission of women to the National University of Ireland', *Education Research and Perspectives*, 35(2), pp 44-56.

HEFCE (Higher Education Funding Council for England) (2014a) 'Differences in degree outcomes'. Available at: www.hefce.ac.uk/pubs/year/2014/201403.

HEFCE (2014b) 'Macroeconomic influences on the demand for part-time higher education in the UK: a report to HEFCE by Oxford Economics'. Available at: www.hefce.ac.uk/media/hefce/content/pubs/indirreports/2014/Macroeconomic,influences,on,the,demand,for,PT,HE/2014_ptdemand.pdf.

HEFCE (2015) 'Differences in degree outcomes: the effect of subject and student characteristics'. Available at: www.hefce.ac.uk/media/HEFCE,2014/Content/Pubs/2015/201521/HEFCE2015_21.pdf.

HESA (Higher Education Statistics Agency) (2018) 'Widening participation: UK performance indicators 2016/17'. Available at: www.hesa.ac.uk/news/01-02-2018/widening-participation-tables.

Hetter, K. (2015) 'New York inmates defeat Harvard debate team', CNN, 7 October. Available at: https://edition.cnn.com/2015/10/07/living/harvard-debate-team-loses-to-prison-inmates-feat/index.html.

Hoare, A. and Johnston, R. (2011) 'Widening participation through admissions policy – a British case study of school and university performance', *Studies in Higher Education*, 36(1), pp 21-41.

Hollis, P. (1998) *Jennie Lee: A life*, Oxford: Oxford University Press.

hooks, b. (1994) *Teaching to transgress*, New York, NY: Routledge.

hooks, b. (2000) *Feminist theory: From margin to center*, London: Pluto Press.

hooks, b. (2003) *Teaching community: A pedagogy of hope*, New York, NY: Routledge.

Horrocks, P. (2017) 'The real casualty of the 2012 tuition fees shake-up? Mature and part-time learners'. Available at: www.universitiesuk.ac.uk/blog/Pages/The-real-casualty-of-2012-tuition-fees-shake-up-mature-and-part-time-learners.aspx.

IPPR (Institute for Public Policy Research) (2017) *Not by degrees: Improving student mental health in UK universities*, London: IPPR.

Johnson, F. (forthcoming) '"Getting off the hill and reaching communities": experience of mature learners as "separate" and "integrated" at an elite university', *Journal of Widening Participation and Lifelong Learning*.

Johnston, R., Manley, D., Jones, K., Harris, R. and Hoare, A. (2015) 'University admissions and the prediction of degree performance: an analysis in the light of changes to the English schools' examination system', *Higher Education Quarterly*, 70(1), pp 24-42.

Jones, B., Moseley, R. and Thomas, G. (2010) *University continuing education 1981–2006: Twenty-five turbulent years*, Leicester: National Institute for Adult and Continuing Education.

Kahneman, D. and Tversky, A. (1972) 'Subjective probability: a judgment of representativeness', *Cognitive Psychology*, 3(3), pp 430-54.

Kumwenda, B., Cleland, J.A., Walker, K., Lee, A.J. and Greatrix, R. (2017) 'The relationship between school type and academic performance at medical school: a national, multi-cohort study', *BMJ open*, 7(8), e016291.

Lagemann, E.C. (2017) 'The continuing challenge of progressive thought: lessons from a college in prison', *Education and Culture*, 33(2), pp 3-11.

Lear, J. (2016) 'Health, well being and adult education'. Available at: https://ec.europa.eu/epale/en/blog/health-well-being-and-adult-education.

Liveley, G. (2006) 'Science fictions and cyber myths: or, do cyborgs dream of Dolly the sheep?', in V. Zajko and E. O'Gorman (eds) *Laughing with Medusa: Classical myth and feminist thought*, Oxford: Oxford University Press, pp 275-94.

Marquetti, A., Schonerwald da Silva, C. and Campbell, A. (2012) 'Participatory economic democracy in action: participatory budget in Porto Alegre, 1989-2004, *Review of Radical Political Economics*, 44(1), pp 62-81.

Marmot, M.G., Allen, J., Goldblatt, P., Boyce, T., McNeish, D., Grady, M. and Geddes, I. (2010) *Fair society, healthy lives: Strategic review of health inequalities in England post-2010*, London: The Marmot Review.

Matthews-King, A. (2017) 'PAs and physios could study medicine part-time to boost doctor numbers', *Pulse*, 19 July. Available at: www.pulsetoday.co.uk/your-practice/practice-topics/education/pas-and-physios-could-study-medicine-part-time-to-boost-doctor-numbers/20034834.article.

McGettigan, A. (2013) *The great university gamble: Money, markets and the future of higher education*, London: Pluto Press.

McLellan, J., Pettigrew, R. and Sperlinger, T. (2016) 'Remaking the elite university: an experiment in widening participation in the UK', *Power and Education*, 8(1), pp 54-72.

McLennan, G. (2008) 'Disinterested, disengaged, useless: conservative or progressive ideas of the university?', *Globalisation, Societies and Education*, 6(2), pp 195-200.

NCCPE (National Co-ordinating Centre for Public Engagement) (undated) 'The history of the National Co-ordinating Centre for Public Engagement'. Available at: www.publicengagement.ac.uk/sites/default/files/publication/history_of_the_nccpe.pdf.

Neary, M. and Amsler, S. (2012) 'Occupy: a new pedagogy of space and time?', *Journal for Critical Education Policy Studies*, 10(2), pp 106-38.

NEF (New Economics Foundation) (2008) *Co-production: A manifesto for growing the core economy*, London: New Economics Foundation.

NUS (National Union of Students) (2016) 'Lost in transition? Provision of mental health support for 16-21 year olds moving to further and higher education', Briefing for All Parliamentary Group on Students. Available at: www.nus.org.uk/PageFiles/2161132/APPG%20on%20Students%20-%20December%20-%20Speaker%20briefing%20-%20Mental%20Health%20(002).pdf.

Nusseibeh, S. (2014) 'Education: capabilities and constraints', *International Journal of Law, Education and Policy*, 10, pp 5-8.

OECD (Organisation for Economic Co-operation and Development) (2017) *OECD Skills Outlook 2017: Skills and global value chains*, Paris: OECD Publishing.

OFFA (Office for Fair Access) (undated), 'Topic briefing: BME students'. Available at: www.offa.org.uk/universities-and-colleges/guidance/topic-briefings/offa-topic-briefing-bme-students.

OFFA (undated) 'Topic briefing: mature learners'. Available at: www.offa.org.uk/universities-and-colleges/guidance/topic-briefings/offa-topic-briefing-mature-learners.

ONS (Office for National Statistics) (2015) *Life expectancy at birth and at aged 65 by local areas in England and Wales: 2012 to 2014*, Newport: ONS.

ONS (2017) 'Annual survey of hours and earnings: 2017 provisional and 2016 revised results'. Available at: www.ons.gov.uk/employmentandlabourmarket/peopleinwork/earningsandworkinghours/bulletins/annualsurveyofhoursandearnings/2017provisionaland2016revisedresults.

O'Shea, S. (2016) 'Avoiding the manufacture of "sameness": first-in-family students, cultural capital and the higher education environment', *Higher Education*, 72(1), pp 59-78.

Palfreyman, D. and Temple, P. (2017) *Universities and colleges: A very short introduction*, Oxford: Oxford University Press.

Philips, I. (2016) '40% of state school teachers never advise students to apply to Oxbridge', *Huffington Post*, 14 October. Available at: www.huffingtonpost.co.uk/entry/state-school-teachers-oxbridge_uk_58008960e4b0e982146c5760.

Raven, P. (2014) 'If doctors can train part time, why not medical students?', *BMJ*, 349, g4897.

Reay, D. (2017) *Miseducation: Inequality, education and the working classes*, Bristol: Policy Press.

Rich, A. (1979) *On lies, secrets and silences: Selected prose 1966-1978*, New York, NY: Norton.

Robertson, A. (2017) 'Over 60 MPs call on minister to commit to adult education resurgence', *FE Week*, 19 January. Available at: https://feweek.co.uk/2017/01/19/over-60-mps-call-on-minister-to-commit-to-adult-education-resurgence.

Rose, J. (2001) *The intellectual life of the British working classes*, New Haven, CT: Yale University Press.

Runciman, D. (2016) 'How the education gap is tearing politics apart', *The Guardian*, 5 October. Available at: www.theguardian.com/politics/2016/oct/05/trump-brexit-education-gap-tearing-politics-apart.

Russell Group (2013) 'Sutton Trust report on access to leading universities'. Available at: http://russell- group.ac.uk/news/sutton-trust-report-on-access-to-leading-universities.

Russell Group (2016) 'Russell Group response to BIS call for evidence: accelerated courses and switch university or degree'. Available at: www.russellgroup.ac.uk/media/5449/russell-group-response-accelerated-courses-and-switching-university-or-degree-july-2016.pdf.

Rustin, S. (2011) 'Should Oxford and Cambridge broaden their intake?', *The Guardian*, 30 April. Available at: www.theguardian.com/education/2011/apr/30/conversation-oxbridge-admissions.

Schuller, T., Preston, J., Hammond, C., Brassett-Grundy, A. and Bynner, J. (2004) *The benefits of learning: The impact of education on health, family life and social capital*, London: Routledge.

Schwab, K. (2016) 'The Fourth Industrial Revolution: what it means, how to respond'. Available at: www.weforum.org/agenda/2016/01/the-fourth-industrial-revolution-what-it-means-and-how-to-respond/.

Silver, N. (2016) 'Education, not income, predicted who would vote for Trump', *FiveThirtyEight*, 22 November. Available at: http://fivethirtyeight.com/features/education-not-income-predicted-who-would-vote-for-trump

Smith, J. and Naylor, R. (2004) 'Schooling effects on subsequent university performance: evidence for the UK university population', *Economics of Education Review*, 24(5), pp 549-62.

Solnit, R. (2010) *A paradise built in hell: The extraordinary communities that arise in disaster*, London: Penguin.

Sperlinger, T. (2012) 'The invisible university: lifelong learning, literary study and the city of Bristol', *Journal of Adult and Continuing Education*, 18 (2), pp 89-96.

Spivak, G.C. (1988) 'Can the subaltern speak?', in C. Nelson and I. Grossberg (eds) *Marxism and the interpretation of culture*, Basingstoke: Macmillan, pp 271-313.

Taylor, R. (2009) 'Lifelong learning under New Labour: an Orwellian dystopia?', *Power and Education*, 1(1), pp 71-82.

Taylor, S., Bell, E., Grugulis, I., Storey, J. and Taylor, L. (2010) 'Politics and power in training and learning: the rise and fall of the NHS university', *Management Learning*, 41(1), pp 89-99.

Thompson, E.P. (1997) *The Romantics: England in a revolutionary age*, New York, NY: Norton.

Tuckett, A. (1991) *Towards a learning workforce: A policy discussion paper on adult learners at work*, Leicester: National Institute of Adult and Continuing Education.

UCAS (Universities and Colleges Admissions Service) (2017) '2017 cycle applicant figures – June deadline'. Available at: https://www.ucas.com/corporate/data-and-analysis/ucas-undergraduate-releases/2017-cycle-applicant-figures-june-deadline-0 (accessed 14 March 2018).

UK Parliament, House of Commons (2018) *Part-time undergraduate students in England*, CBP 796626, London: House of Commons.

UK Parliament, House of Commons Exiting the European Union Committee (2018) 'EU exit analysis cross Whitehall briefing'. Available at: www.parliament.uk/documents/commons-committees/Exiting-the-European-Union/17-19/Cross-Whitehall-briefing/EU-Exit-Analysis-Cross-Whitehall-Briefing.pdf.

UNESCO (United Nations Educational, Scientific and Cultural Organization) (2017) *Six ways to ensure higher education leaves no-one behind*, Paris: UNESCO.

Universities UK (2017) *Patterns and trends in UK higher education 2017*, London: Universities UK.

Wainwright, H. (2003) *Reclaim the state: experiments in popular democracy*, London: Verso.

Warikoo, N.K. (2016) *The diversity bargain, and other dilemmas of race, admissions and meritocracy at elite universities*, Chicago, IL and London: University of Chicago Press.

Watson, D. (2009) 'Foundations, funding and forgetfulness: reflections on the pattern of university histories', in P. Cunningham with S. Oosthuizen and R. Taylor (eds) *Beyond the lecture hall: Universities and community engagement from the middle ages to the present day*, Cambridge: Cambridge University Press, pp 9-18.

WEF (World Economic Forum) (2017) *Accelerating workforce reskilling for the Fourth Industrial Revolution: an agenda for leaders to shape the future of education, gender and work*, Geneva: WEF.

Wilby, P. (2014) 'Alan Tuckett: the man who invented the "adult learner"', *The Guardian,* 21 October. Available at: www.theguardian.com/education/2014/oct/21/man-invented-adult-learner-alan-tuckett.

Wilby, P. (2018) 'A visionary to save the Open University – or the man who will run it into the ground?', *The Guardian*, 9 January. Available at: www.theguardian.com/education/2018/jan/09/save-open-university-peter-horrocks-changing.

Willetts, D. (2017) *A university education*, Oxford: Oxford University Press.

Williams, R. (1961) *The long revolution*, London: Chatto & Windus.

Willis, I. (2017) *Reception*, New York, NY: Routledge.

Young, M.D. (1958) *The rise of the meritocracy, 1870-2033: An essay on education and equality*, London: Thames & Hudson.

Index

References to figures and tables are in *italics*. References to notes are the page number followed by 'n' then the note number (eg. 170n16)